Papers in Contrastive Linguistics

Papers in Contrastive Linguistics

EDITED BY

GERHARD NICKEL

Professor of English Linguistics and Philology
University of Stuttgart

CAMBRIDGE

at the University Press 1971

Published by the Syndics of the Cambridge University Press
Bentley House, 200 Euston Road, London NW1 2DB
American Branch: 32 East 57th Street, New York, N.Y.10022

© Cambridge University Press 1971

Library of Congress Catalogue Card Number: 78–149434

ISBN: 0 521 08091 6

Printed in Great Britain
at the University Printing House, Cambridge
(Brooke Crutchley, University Printer)

Contents

44806

[v]

Preface

One of the largest sections at the Second International Conference of Applied Linguistics, held in Cambridge between 8 and 9 September 1969 and most capably organized by the British Association for Applied Linguistics (BAAL) on behalf of the Association Internationale de Linguistique Appliquée (AILA), was devoted to the field of contrastive linguistics. I had the privilege both of acting as leader to this section and of presenting a paper on contrastive linguistics and language teaching to the Plenary Session.

When the organizing committee subsequently asked me to edit a selection of papers read in my section, I accepted the flattering invitation in the hope of thus being able to offer a further small personal contribution to this important area of research within the vast field of applied linguistics.

It is to be regretted that limitations of space have compelled me to omit some interesting papers. I wish to offer my thanks to BAAL, and to Mr John G. Trim in particular, for the idea and the invitation to produce this volume. My thanks are also due to the Cambridge University Press for their friendly cooperation and for displaying much patience. Finally, I should like to record my appreciation to Ekkehard König for rendering indispensable editorial assistance.

It is my hope that the present volume may help to promote further fruitful discussion throughout the world on topics of contrastive linguistics, particularly where these relate to foreign-language teaching.

G. N.

May 1971

Introduction

This collection of papers from the Contrastive Linguistics Section at the Second International Conference of Applied Linguistics provides evidence of world-wide scholarly interest in the analysis of correspondences and discrepancies between a variety of source and target languages.

Several papers, particularly those in the field of phonology, claim that neither so-called classical phonemics nor generative phonology are entirely adequate instruments for predicting interference phenomena. Consequently, some authors have proposed modifications in the models they use. By and large the generative-transformational model in its various forms still seems to predominate in most of the work represented here. One paper, however, advocates a stratificational approach in contrastive analysis. Whichever model or framework they employ, all authors seem to be in agreement on one point of methodology: that one and the same approach should be used within one and the same investigation. In some papers and in ensuing discussions it was suggested that, in view of the urgent need for material which can be converted into pedagogically optimate format, older and more widely known frameworks of language description might be more useful than current models for some kinds of comparative work. This is undoubtedly true. Which theoretical framework is chosen, should depend ultimately on one's objectives. The use of traditional descriptions will certainly lead to quicker results. A danger inherent in more sophisticated theoretical frameworks such as transformational-generative grammar is that the proponent of such models may easily lose sight of the practical aims he had in mind when starting his investigation. However, the results of more formal and explicit approaches may well be more impressive in the long run.

The contributions also seem to show that applied linguistics is not viable without theories. The authors, however, usually appear willing to modify theory in the light of empirical data. This scientific standpoint ensures that contrastive linguistics will not become estranged from the field of pedagogic practice.

Several papers, with some justification, call for greater emphasis to be given to empirical studies. The papers in question are concerned with the practical investigation of transfer phenomena. They draw attention to certain problems of transfer from source to target language, a theme that is far from having been completely exhausted. The authors deal with language interference in the fields of phonology and of syntax, and some interesting phenomena are described here.

Other papers deal more directly with a very important aspect of applied linguistics, foreign-language teaching. Here several authors discuss the important problems of designing teaching material based on sound linguistic progression and of grading material. Needless to say, the authors agree that contrastive linguistics is not the only way towards a solution of these highly complex problems. Undoubtedly, however, this is a field of particular interest to teachers of foreign languages.

Most contributors are also keenly interested in the implications their work may have for areas outside language teaching. Contrastive linguistics, of course, also has a bearing on such topics as language typology. It is evident from some papers that the findings of contrastive analyses are also of use in general linguistic investigations and in the study of language universals. One paper, for instance, utilizes contrastive material in treating the problem of the reliability of grammaticality judgements made by native speakers. The value and significance of contrastive linguistics was also demonstrated by reports on the various projects now under way. A worldwide network of research in contrastive analysis seems to be arising. It is to be hoped that agreement on coordinating projects and cooperation in the exchange of information will be made possible at an early date. The degree to which contrastive linguistics overlaps with other branches of linguistic research – for instance, with error analysis – became apparent during the conference: some papers in this section treat topics which could have been presented with equal justification in other sections; other sections dealt with themes of relevance to' contrastive linguistics. Perhaps this question of coordination can be taken account of at future conferences on applied linguistics.

In general the conference has shown that the theory of contrastive analysis is still in a state of flux. There is at present a need for further broad and detailed studies of an empirical kind. Until such studies are forthcoming we are bound to be faced with a certain amount of scepticism concerning the overall usefulness of contrastive analysis. The papers read at the conference and the contributions made in the ensuing lively discussions all displayed the sense of modesty appropriate in view of the present state of the art. Participants and contributors, I think, were all only too aware that there are more things in language than are dreamt of in our linguistics – contrastive or otherwise.

Contrastive linguistics and foreign-language teaching

GERHARD NICKEL

The role of applied contrastive linguistics must be seen in connection with overall endeavours to rationalize foreign-language teaching. It must also be dealt with within the general framework of school-teaching. New subjects claim a place in school curricula. Foreign-language teaching must be intensified since it has not always produced the results hoped for. A reduction in the number of foreign languages taught is hardly feasible, seeing that the importance of the major West European languages, English, French, German and Spanish, is being increasingly recognized and their teaching encouraged by important official bodies. The Council of Europe, for instance, has set up a number of special programmes to promote the teaching and dissemination of European languages. Since the number of school hours available for teaching foreign languages is limited, it will be necessary to introduce some forms of rationalization in language-teaching programmes. One way of doing so will be to introduce new teaching methods such as programmed instruction, a method with a big future. A further way will be the utilization of technical devices, e.g. audio-visual aids. Finally, use will be made of certain findings of modern linguistic science, particularly of that small branch of it known as contrastive linguistics.

At this point a few words on the term 'contrastive linguistics' and the history of the subject may not be out of place. Comparing individual languages is, of course, nothing new. On the one hand we have the well-established discipline of comparative philology – a branch of learning which may be said to have reached its zenith in nineteenth-century Germany. However, the aims and methods of comparative philology differ considerably from those of contrastive linguistics. The comparativist compares languages in order to trace their phylogenetic relationships. He may attempt to reconstruct the putative parent language from which kindred languages are thought to have descended. The material he draws on for comparison consists in the main of individual sounds and words. Contrastive linguistics, on the other hand, for the most part compares languages with the quite utilitarian aim of improving the methods and results of language teaching. Its comparisons range over a wider area of language structure than those of traditional comparative philology and its methods differ accordingly. We shall say more about this later.

Before leaving the topic 'comparative philology' mention should be made of a rather different approach to language comparison, though one still to some extent within the traditional comparativist framework, that of the famous Prague School, whose founder, V. Mathesius, recognized the importance of contrastive linguistics very clearly. In this case the construction and function of languages are compared, with the aid of so-called analytic procedures, in order to learn more about the system of one's own language.

Contrastive linguistics is not merely relevant for foreign-language teaching. It can make useful contributions to machine translation and linguistic typology. However, the possibilities in this direction have not been fully explored and have no direct bearing on our theme.

In foreign-language teaching at school the contrastive approach is not completely new either. It is reflected, for instance, in the classroom use of such terms as 'Gallicism', 'Germanism' and 'Anglicism'. However, it is usually only lexical phenomena which have been compared, and systematic contrastive analyses are not made use of in traditional language instruction.

Contrastive linguistics as a systematic branch of linguistic science is of fairly recent date – though it is not really the idea as such which is new, but rather the systematization. The publication in 1957 of Robert Lado's *Linguistics across Cultures* marks the real beginning of modern applied contrastive linguistics. Lado on the first page of his book quotes Charles C. Fries, the American structuralist who took the lead in applying the principles of linguistic science to the teaching of English. On the role of contrastive linguistics Fries says: 'The most effective materials are those that are based upon a scientific description of the language to be learned, carefully compared with a parallel description of the native language of the learner.'[1] Lado supports this contention with the following words: 'Textbooks should be graded as to grammatical structure, pronunciation, vocabulary, and cultural content. And grading can be done best after the kind of comparison we are presenting here' (p. 3). Two years later work

---

[1] C. C. Fries, *Teaching and Learning English as a Foreign Language* (Ann Arbor, 1945), p. 9. Cf. also R. L. Politzer, *Teaching French* (Waltham, Mass. [cop.]², 1965).

was started on the *Contrastive Structure Series,* edited by Charles A. Ferguson under the auspices of the Center for Applied Linguistics of the Modern Language Association of America in Washington, D.C. The series has as its aim the description of similarities and differences between English and each of the five foreign languages most commonly taught in the U.S.A.: French, German, Italian, Russian and Spanish. To date, the volumes on German, Italian and Spanish have appeared.[1]

In the meantime work in the field of contrastive linguistics has steadily increased. At present research projects are under way in Poznań (Polish–English), Zagreb (Serbo-Croatian–English), Bucharest (Rumanian–English), An Teanglann (Irish–English), Stuttgart (German–English), as well as at other centres. The Stuttgart Project on Applied Contrastive Linguistics (PAKS), of which I am the director, is being generously supported by the Volkswagen Foundation and has also received a contribution from the State Government of Baden-Württemberg.

It is symptomatic of the current interest in contrastive linguistics that the Nineteenth Round Table Meeting at Georgetown University, Washington, in 1968 was devoted exclusively to 'Contrastive Linguistics and its Pedagogical Implications'.[2] Problems of contrastive linguistics were also on the agenda at the 1969 Spring Conference of the Institute for the German Language at Mannheim. In January 1971 the Pacific Conference on Contrastive Linguistics and Language Universals will take place in Honolulu.

There is little need to emphasize that progress in this field would be furthered if close cooperation between the various centres working on contrastive studies were made possible. The Council of Europe has entrusted our Stuttgart Institute with the registration of projects within its domain. We hope to make an inventory of the most important work in progress or planned and should welcome information from research centres and individual scholars.

We have already pointed out that the idea of contrasting languages for teaching purposes is not new. Traditional foreign-language grammars make use of the contrastive approach when they compare constructions or

---

[1] W. G. Moulton, *The Sounds of English and German* (Chicago, 1962); H. L. Kufner, *The Grammatical Structures of English and German* (Chicago, 1962); R. P. Stockwell and J. D. Bowen, *The Sounds of English and Spanish* (Chicago, 1965); R. P. Stockwell, J. D. Bowen and J. W. Martin, *The Grammatical Structures of English and Spanish* (Chicago, 1965); F. B. Agard and R. J. Di Pietro, *The Sounds of English and Italian* (Chicago, 1966) and *The Grammatical Structures of English and Italian* (Chicago, 1966).
[2] 'Contrastive linguistics and its pedagogical implications'. In: J. E. Alatis (ed.), *Report of the Nineteenth Annual Round Table Meeting on Linguistics and Language Studies, Monograph Series on Languages and Linguistics* No. 21 (Washington, 1968).

functions of the target language with those of the source language. Such comparisons within the framework of traditional grammar have turned out to be quite useful for pedagogical purposes; however, they suffer from a general defect: the traditional grammar on which they are based is not sufficiently explicit to permit exact analyses.

The first studies in the *Contrastive Structure Series* went a step beyond traditional grammarians by using as their frame of reference the taxonomic model of language developed in the U.S.A. during the so-called Bloomfieldian era (early 1930s to mid-1950s). The linguist using this model takes as his starting point a corpus of generated utterances; he then seeks to establish the elements of which the utterances consist (e.g. phonemes and morphemes) and to state the distribution of these elements relative to each other. The use of this model in contrastive analyses led to many useful insights. Here again, however, the model was not adequate enough to permit really detailed contrastive analyses of languages.[1]

The latest studies in the *Contrastive Structure Series* are based on the transformational-generative (TG) model of language as developed since around 1957 by N. A. Chomsky, Z. S. Harris and others. This model is also being employed as the frame of reference in the PAKS investigation at Stuttgart. In the course of our work it has become clear that the use of an explicit language model can bring to light various features of language structure which would probably have otherwise remained hidden. On the other hand, features of language structure revealed in a contrastive analysis may suggest modifications of the model. The TG model has been subjected to several modifications and will certainly be further modified in the light of future experience. Any explicit language model can be employed as a framework for a contrastive investigation. We are using TG grammar as this is at present the most fully developed model of language, but we are remaining open-minded towards analyses using models other than TG (e.g. stratificational grammar and tagmemics) in the knowledge that it is a grammar of performance rather than a grammar of competence that applied contrastive linguistics employed for error analysis should be based upon.

What are some advantages of using TG grammar in a contrastive analysis? One advantage is that differences between languages are formulated as differences between systems and domains of rules. This approach often reveals divergences much finer than those detectable by previous methods of description. (Of course, formulations of divergences in terms of rules

---

[1] Cf. G. Nickel, 'Der moderne Strukturalismus und seine Weiterführung bis zur generativen Transformationsgrammatik', *Neusprachliche Mitteilungen* 21 (1968), 5–15.

are also employed in generative models making no use of transformations.) A further advantage is the conception of 'deep structure' and 'surface structure' in TG. In the light of this notion many structural differences between source and target language turn out to be merely superficial: a deep-structure feature common to both languages may be manifested differently in the surface structure of the languages and vice versa. This is true of the case systems in German and English as will be demonstrated below.[1] This brings us to the question of the applicability of results of research to teaching practice – a consideration which must always remain foremost in the mind of the applied linguist conducting a contrastive investigation. It is in part up to the psychologist to ascertain the extent to which the notion of a deep structure common to several languages can be utilized to make language learning easier. The results of some investigations point in this direction. A further point in favour of using TG in contrastive investigations is the current preoccupation of TG grammarians with linguistic universals, i.e. with linguistic statements which include all languages in their scope.

Naturally, increasingly refined ways of dealing with certain aspects of TG grammar, in particular with its semantic component, can have, if justified, implications for its application in contrastive linguistics.[2] However, we shall not deal with these points now since, as previously mentioned, contrastive linguistics is not dependent on any particular model: as far as models are concerned it simply requires a uniform framework of comparison.

A further problem connected with contrastive linguistics is that of 'equivalence'. Whereas formal equivalence can be established relatively easily, it is a most difficult problem to set up any kind of functional-semantic equivalence. Since individual languages possess systems and subsystems peculiar to themselves, every function and construction within the language must be regarded as a part of the whole. We cannot go into this problem either since it is in principle incapable of solution. Probably the best one can do is to take a pragmatic view and approach it by way of a notion of 'quasi-equivalence' with approximate values, as is done in the field of translation.

[1] C. J. Fillmore, 'A proposal concerning English prepositions'. In: F. P. Dineen (ed.), *Report of the Seventeenth Annual Round Table Meeting on Linguistics and Language Studies, Monograph Series on Languages and Linguistics* No. 19 (Washington, 1966). Cf. also E. König und G. Nickel, 'Transformationelle Restriktionen in der Verbalsyntax des Englischen und Deutschen'. In: *Probleme der kontrastiven Sprachwissenschaft. Jahrbuch 1969 des Instituts für Deutsche Sprache* (Düsseldorf, 1970).
[2] R. P. Stockwell, 'Contrastive analysis and lapsed time'. In: *Monograph Series on Languages and Linguistics* No. 21, pp. 11–26.

Neither theoretical nor applied contrastive linguistics can offer more that a partial contribution to the planning of foreign-language teaching. It is probable that the influence of applied contrastive linguistics will be greater on the designing of teaching programmes for adults than on those for children. The reason is that in the teaching of adults more use can be made of the learners' better-developed cognitive faculties. In general, however, we regard contrastive linguistics as being relevant to the designing of teaching material for use in all age groups. The practical application of such results will also make it necessary for teachers of the target language to have a knowledge of the structure of the source language. In particular it will be textbooks and teaching materials that will take account of the structure of the source language. Here it must be emphasized once again that contrastive linguistics does not provide the only criterion for the designing of textbooks. Many other factors must be taken into account here, e.g. age and sex of pupils, teaching objectives (including the question of specialist languages), the psychology of learning, motivation, etc.).

It should be pointed out that contrastive linguistics is not opposed to the so-called 'direct method'. On the contrary, since it recognizes the powerful influence of the source language in the learning of a second language, it will recommend the intensive use of the target language in foreign-language teaching.

Of course, contrastive linguistics has its critics. Let me cite just one example:

The major contribution of the linguist to language teaching was seen as an intensive contrastive study of the systems of the second language and the mother-tongue of the learner...Teachers have not always been very impressed by this contribution from the linguist for the reason that their practical experience has usually already shown them where these difficulties lie and they have not felt that the contribution of the linguist has provided them with any significantly new information. They noted for example that many of the errors with which they were familiar were not predicted by the linguist anyway.[1]

This noteworthy statement calls for the following comment: in the first place, it must, of course, be conceded that many foreign-language teachers have long recognized difficulties caused by interference from the source language. However, on the one hand, it does not hold good for all teachers, and on the other hand a systematic comparison of two language systems permits of a finer grading of difficulties. In the second place, contrastive linguistics is not at all committed to the view that all mistakes made by learners of foreign languages are caused by interference from the source

---

[1] S. P. Corder, 'The significance of learner's errors', *IRAL* 5 (1967), 162.

language. Mistakes may, of course, also arise from the fact that the system of the target language is not impressed with sufficient firmness on the learner's memory – a situation which leads to the intrastructural confusing and conflation of distinct rules of the target language (e.g. in the form of over-generalization of new rules, hypercorrectness, etc.). There is, of course, also interstructural interference between target languages. Finally, mistakes may have 'physiological' and 'psychological' origins, e.g. lack of attention from extra-linguistic causes and linguistically motivated inattentiveness should be clearly discriminated. The linguist is not responsible for predicting errors of the latter kind. It must be constantly emphasized that the contribution of contrastive linguistics to the design of teaching programmes is only a partial one and that predicting errors is not its only task. However, to maintain, as two linguists have done, that teaching material designed on a contrastive basis is more likely to hinder than to help in the learning of a second language surely runs counter to all the available evidence.[1] Other factors must, of course, be taken into account in preparing teaching materials. These other factors include, for example, the purposeful contextualization of examples.

In order to make clear the significance of contrastive linguistics it will be appropriate to say here something about the process of learning a language. The following diagram is a schematic representation of the communication process involved in child language learning when only the first language is involved:

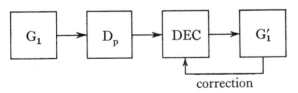

correction

G_1 = grammar of source language D_p = primary linguistic data
DEC = decoding G_1' = acquired grammar[2]

The process of learning the first language is certainly neither economical nor simple. The fact that it is nevertheless successful is due to the strong motivation at play, the large amount of 'teaching effort' involved (e.g. on the part of parents, brothers and sisters, playmates, etc.), and the usually clear relationships between the primary linguistic data and the situational

[1] L. Newmark and D. Reibel, 'Necessity and sufficiency in language learning', *IRAL* 6 (1968), 145–64. One of the merits of this article, however, undoubtedly lies in its sound warning against overrating the role of contrastive analyses in foreign-language teaching.
[2] G. Nickel, 'Rationalisierung des Fremdsprachenunterrichts', *Paedagogica Europaea* 4 (1968), 85–97.

context. This model may possibly still to some extent reflect the learning situation when a second language is being acquired, but only if the language is learned in a speech community of native speakers under conditions approaching those holding when a first language is learned. However, even in such cases, and also in the case of so-called bilingualism in early childhood, a modification of the model is probably called for. Perhaps I should mention in passing that I do not think that both languages have perfectly equal status in cases of bilingualism, i.e. a bilingual speaker is probably never equally competent in both languages. The brain seems to have difficulty in storing the data of the different languages separately. If there is a degree of overlapping even between the languages in bilingual communities, this is one further justification for the contrastive analysis of languages.

Since we wish to deal with the learning of foreign languages in the speech community of the source language, i.e. under normal classroom conditions, our language-acquisition model will have to be modified somewhat. The learner is confronted this time not with primary linguistic data of the mother tongue but with secondary linguistic data of the target language, data which have been prepared by didactic and methodic programming. By 'didactic programming' we understand the manipulation of the linguistic data of the target language, and by 'methodic programming' we understand in general the presentation of the linguistic data in accordance with pedagogical principles. Didactic programming determines *what* is to be taught, methodic programming determines *how* it is to be taught. A further point to be taken into account is the fact that the learner of a second language has already acquired a language system, which is a possible source of interference. The communication process involved in acquiring a second language under classroom conditions may be represented schematically as follows:

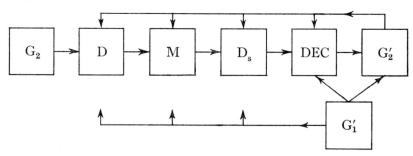

G_1' = grammar of source language G_2 = grammar of target language
D_s = secondary linguistic data   D = didactic programming
M = methodic programming   DEC = decoding
G_2' = acquired grammar of target language

The aim of a contrastive analysis of two languages is the description of a partial grammar G_C which is made up of the sum of the differences between the grammar of the source language (G_1') and that of the target language (G_2). This differential grammar is the focus of the didactic programming. That does not, of course, imply that corresponding sections of the two grammatical systems should not be taught. Such a step would inevitably lead towards a distorted view of the target language on the learner's part. At all events, this partial grammar will influence the selection and grading of the teaching material, thus also determining the staging of instruction and the sequencing of the material used.[1]

Once again it must be emphasized that the results of contrastive analyses are not the only factors to be considered in designing teaching materials. Modern foreign-language teaching must be up to date in all respects. Dialogues, for instance, must deal with modern topics in a modern manner. It will often be necessary to build into the programme at an early stage very difficult linguistic expressions which must nevertheless be included on account of their high frequency. As instances one could mention the so-called irregular verbs and constructions such as the English 'tag question', which – unlike its German or French equivalent – is not always easy for foreigners to learn. Here, as elsewhere, we must strive for compromises.

The first objective of PAKS has been an investigation of the basic problems of interlinguistic comparison. It is difficult to predict whether it will ever be possible to set up a general theory of linguistic interference. So far studies have been made on the adjective, adverb, verb, relative clause and on certain sectors of lexicology. Some of the studies have appeared in PAKS reports (Nos. 1–5); others are being written as masters', doctoral and habilitation theses.

The final objective of all PAKS investigations is a reference grammar of English and German, which is intended to provide a comprehensive guide for the designing of classroom teaching material for all levels.

Another aim of PAKS is the grading of teaching material according to degree of difficulty. 'Difficulty', of course, is a controversial notion. Nevertheless, what we have said on this theme in another publication still holds good:

Although one can discover by long observation what errors are likely to occur, a contrastive analysis goes beyond such mere listing because it may provide an explanation of why such mistakes are made, how great their degree of difficulty is and which steps must be undertaken to avoid them.[2]

---

[1] For these terms cf. M. A. K. Halliday, A. McIntosh and P. Strevens, *The Linguistic Sciences and Language Teaching* (London, 1964), p. 204 ff.

[2] G. Nickel and K. H. Wagner, 'Contrastive linguistics and language teaching', *IRAL* 6 (1968), 247.

R. P. Stockwell and G. D. Bowen have already attempted to establish on a linguistic basis a hierarchy of difficulty in pronunciation (the target language was Spanish, the source language English). Using three basic criteria (non-existence, optional and obligatory presence of phonological units in source and target language), they set up a system with eight ranks.[1] Most difficult to learn are phonological phenomena which, though not present in the source language, are obligatory in the target language. At the other end of the scale of difficulty are phonological forms which in both languages are subject to obligatory rules. This linguistic scale is much too coarse-meshed and to some extent arbitrary. It also shows that practical teaching does not merely depend on linguistic data. Thus it by no means inevitably follows that the non-presence of a sound feature in the target language automatically places this feature in the category 'most difficult'. Systematic psychological investigations into this problem have not yet been undertaken, nevertheless we already know that considerable distinctions must be made. On the one hand, the learner's age will be influential. At an early age, when the child's imitative drive is strong and when it takes an especial pleasure in making discoveries, a completely unfamiliar sound of the target language is often more easily acquired than one differing only in distribution (e.g. German initial /z/ compared with English /s/). A further point determining the difficulty of a sound is whether it can be made visible as can the English interdental fricatives /ð/ and /θ/. This is another field of experimentation for linguistics and the psychology of learning.

Attempts have also been made to set up a complicated scale of difficulty for syntax.[2] It comprises sixteen ranks and takes into account structural and semantic equivalence in addition to the factors mentioned in connection with the phonological hierarchy. Naturally, the situation in syntax is more complicated than that of phonology. Here again the scale turns out to be somewhat arbitrary and too coarse-meshed, a fact which is accentuated by the presence of partial equivalences (e.g. English and German perfect tense) holding between individual syntactic constructions in various languages. At the top of the hierarchy of difficulty where the German learner of English is concerned we find the English do-periphrasis, the reason being that this kind of construction does not occur in German, at least not in the standard language. Once again it is the task of the teacher to establish by tests whether the scale of linguistic difficulty construed on a logical basis corresponds to analogous difficulties on the part of the learner. It

[1] R. P. Stockwell and J. D. Bowen, *The Sounds of English and Spanish*, p. 16.
[2] R. P. Stockwell, J. D. Bowen and J. W. Martin, *The Grammatical Structures of English and Spanish*, p. 284.

seems to us that in the field of syntax correspondences may well be closer than in the field of phonology. At all events, an interesting beginning has been made.[1]

Some use at least can be made of such a scale of difficulty in designing teaching material. Moreover, it cannot be entirely disregarded in the evaluation of mistakes. The problem of evaluating mistakes is, of course, a very complex one. It cannot be solved on a purely linguistic basis: pedagogical considerations must be taken into account, too. We are dealing here with interdisciplinary territory where linguists and teachers could cooperate to good advantage. The least result to be expected from such cooperation would be more objective criteria for error evaluation than have been hitherto in use. It should, for instance, be clear that errors based on contrastive interference should be judged with lenience and understanding in an early stage of language learning. The question must be approached from various sides, and care must be taken to avoid overemphasizing the approach of any one group such as the linguistic one.[2] At all events, it cannot be denied that linguistics is justified in attempting to make a contribution to the solution of this very complex problem. Error analysis and contrastive analysis do not exclude, but on the contrary complement each other: the former covers more than only contrastive relations, the latter tries not only to describe errors, but also to analyse one particular source in detail.[3] Whether one starts with error analysis and then proceeds to a contrastive analysis, or vice versa, is a question of method and objective.

Obvious differences between the rule systems of different languages have always aroused the interest of grammarians. One merely has to recall typical chapters of English grammars written for Germans, e.g. 'Gerund', 'Accusative with Infinitive', 'Nominative with Infinitive', 'Progressive Form', 'Phrasal Verbs', etc. Structural comparisons are primarily concerned with general differences and correspondences, those which apply to more than one instance. One is here interested in at least semi-productive rules. It is sometimes possible to take from the very broad and often vaguely demarcated field of 'idioms' numerous phenomena which on account of their regular character can be assigned to the area of systematic grammar. An example: of the English pair *the language of description* and *the language*

---

[1] Cf. also L. Dušková, 'On sources of errors in foreign language learning', *IRAL* 7 (1969), 11–30; B. H. Banathy and P. H. Madarasz, 'Contrastive analysis and error analysis', *Journal of English as a Second Language* 4 (1969), 77–92.

[2] W. R. Lee, 'Thoughts on contrastive linguistics in the context of language teaching'. In: *Monograph Series on Languages and Linguistics* No. 21, pp. 185–94.

[3] For relations between contrastive linguistics and error analysis cf. *PAKS-Report* No. 5, part of which has been published by F. Cornelsen Verlag K.G. (Berlin, 1971).

under description only the first has an 'analogous' equivalent in German, *die Sprache der Beschreibung*, but *die Sprache, die beschrieben wird*. In English the phrase *the language under description* comes under the domination of a group of verbs including *comment, compare, consider, debate, discuss, examine*, etc. Equivalent rules often have different domains. Thus in German only the structure NP_1–VP–NP_2 (in which $NP_2 =$ direct object) comes under the domain of the passive transformation; in English, on the other hand, the passive transformation can also be applied to indirect objects (e.g. after *give, lend, offer, sell, send, show*) and prepositional objects. Traditional grammar recognized this too.

Apart from the problem of the equivalence of structures, there is also the question of acceptability, which overlaps a good deal with the field of stylistics. We still need extensive contrastive investigations into these problems. However, most will no doubt agree that the central areas of linguistic systems should be dealt with before these more peripheral regions. As an example of this sliding scale of different degrees of acceptability between English and German we might cite pronominalization in copula sentences (this phenomenon is less usual in German than in English):

The committee's suggestion that...is a good one. *Das Problem, dem wir uns gegenübersehen, ist ein schwieriges.*

We pointed out above that numerous differences between language systems do not become apparent until the languages are viewed in the light of an explicit model. Giving due regard to reservations one may have with regard to certain developments in TG grammar, it appears nevertheless undeniable that the model has thrown light on many aspects of language. This holds good, for instance, for the conception of case as developed by C. J. Fillmore.[1] Fillmore starts with the assumption that such functional notions as 'subject' and 'object' refer to phenomena of the syntactic surface structure. The function in the sentence of nominal elements which are semantically relevant and which determine the valence of a verb is regarded by Fillmore as being determined by a set of abstract deep-structure units, each of which stands in a given syntactic-semantic relation to the verb. Thus Fillmore distinguishes such functions as A(gentive), O(bject), I(nstrumental), D(ative), L(ocative), which he calls, following Tesnière, 'actants'. The valence of a verb is determined by the number and type of actants with which it can occur in grammatical sentences. Thus the English verb *open* has the following features: $/ \!\!-\!\!-\!\! O\,(I)\,(A)\,/$. Under certain circumstances any actant can be the subject of a sentence containing the

[1] Cf. C. J. Fillmore, 'A proposal concerning English prepositions'.

verb *open* although, of course, stylistic and other restrictions may play a part.[1]

In the sentence

/The room/$_L$ is hot

it is apparent that a number of predicates permit locative actants as a subject. The paraphrase

It is hot /in the room/$_L$

shows that the NP *the room* must be regarded as a locative in the deep structure, different from 'the milk is hot', where such a paraphrase would hardly be possible, though it must be admitted that these are examples where case distinctions of this deep-structure type break down.

Using this model, one can show that in the selection of inanimate subjects German is subject to more restrictions in such cases than English.[2] Thus in the case of many verb groups it is possible in English, but not in German, to place instrumentals, locatives (and objectives) at the head of active sentences, the actants in the head position thereby becoming subjects.

This diversity in the selection of subjects is manifested, for instance, when instrumentals are given front position. An English verb group displaying this kind of diversity is the group of dative verbs which includes *earn, gain, get, save, gross, lose, make, net, obtain, realize, win*. The corresponding German verbs do not normally permit instrumentals in subject position. Of course, the problem of acceptability arises here again. Perhaps the English sentence

This bet won me £100

could be rendered in German by

Diese Wette brachte mir £100 ein.

Usually, however, the latter sentence will give way to

Mit (durch diese) dieser Wette gewann ich £100.

A number of verbs expressing the extermination, destruction, injuring or damaging of animate or inanimate objects (e.g. English *damage, drown, fracture, injure, kill, shatter, smash, stunt*) are subject to similar restrictions in English and German (here, too, questions of style may have to be considered). In general the English sentence

The accident killed many people

---

[1] Cf. E. König and G. Nickel. 'Transformationnelle Restriktionen in der Verbalsyntax des Englischen und Deutschen'.

[2] For vague and too general statements cf. J. Gelhard, *Englische Stillehre* (Wiesbaden, 1956), p. 21 ff.

will be rendered by the German

Bei (durch den) dem Unfall wurden viele Menschen getötet.

In German an instrumental with subject function would be rather unusual.
English is also more liberal than German in giving front position and
subject function to locatives. A rather heterogenous group of English verbs
like *drown, feed, grow, hide, seat, see, show, sleep*, etc. and the corresponding
verbs in German demonstrate this.

How delicate the syntactic behaviour of individual verbs within this
group may be is demonstrated by the examples of *seat* and *sleep*. These
verbs permit front position of the locative only if the agentive is made
object and at the same time 'quantified':

This aircraft seats 100 people.

In diesem Flugzeug können 100 Personen Platz finden.

This tent sleeps four people.

In diesem Zelt können vier Personen schlafen.

Here the delicacy of TG grammar once again becomes apparent. Some of
the distinctions which are brought to light are rather too fine to be utilized
for pedagogical purposes. A simplification is necessary if the material is to
be used for classroom purposes. But it would not be the first time in the
history of grammars that a comprehensive scientific grammar has given
rise to a smaller, handier version for teaching and learning purposes. One
only need to recall O. Jespersen's *Modern English Grammar* (*MEG*) and
his *Essentials of English Grammar*.

At all events, these few examples will have made clear that a new instrument of investigation, e.g. a new notion of case, can bring to light certain
features of language and represent them with a hitherto unknown precision.
From this position the road is open for typological studies which are also
founded on new notions. Stylistics, too, in which so much has hitherto
been based on intuition, will have a more explicit basis.

Lexicology is another field which will receive fresh impulses from a more
exact contrastive analysis. Naturally, every dictionary like every grammar
is in a sense built upon contrastive principles. An important point is the
selection of the systematic criteria according to which the contrastive
analysis is carried out. Most dictionaries have been compiled in a very
arbitrary fashion, and the distinction of meanings in the various languages
treated is not made in accordance with uniform principles. Contrastive
analyses in lexicology will by no means be a simple matter. Here again it
may turn out that the network of the componential parameters necessary
for distinguishing meanings will be too close-meshed for pedagogical pur-

poses and that dictionaries used in teaching will have to make a judicious selection of results achieved in pure research.

In contrastive analyses the unity of register must also be observed. Register is a factor which must in future be given greater attention than hitherto. It can be repeatedly observed that there is a clearer separation of registers in this age of specialization than heretofore. The problem of specialist languages, which have to be compared with one another, crops up here, too.

J. B. Carroll, looking at contrastive linguistics from the point of view of the psychology of learning, takes a positive view of the subject.[1] He and others have recently called attention again to the well-known fact of inter-lingual convergences and divergences.[2] We know that from the lexico-logical point of view English is largely divergent relative to German. This also holds good for areas of syntax, e.g. the tense and aspect systems. This phenomenon will be further elucidated by a more detailed contrastive analysis. The psychologist will be interested in the relationship between convergence and divergence phenomena and the learning process. It is apparent that convergence phenomena are advantageous in encoding, but disadvantageous in decoding. This fact, therefore, has different implications according to whether active or passive language skills are to be taught.

By way of summary, let us point out once again that applied contrastive linguistics does not aim at drawing the pupils' attention constantly and systematically to language contrasts. Its objective, rather, is to aid the textbook author in collecting and arranging his material and to help the teacher in presenting his subject-matter. Both author and teacher require a knowledge of contrastive grammar in order to be able to predict, explain, correct, and eliminate errors due to interference between source and target language. The effect of contrastive linguistics in teaching practice will vary accordingly to teaching objectives and age of the learners. Not all the results of contrastive analyses will be utilizable for practical work.

Contrastive linguistics will also have a part to play in the evaluation of errors. However, the problems of foreign-language teaching will certainly not be solved by contrastive linguistics alone. The psychology of learning will also have to contribute to the investigation of interference phenomena since the latter may well be highly idiosyncratic in many cases. The

---

[1] J. B. Carroll, 'Contrastive linguistics and interference theory'. In: *Monograph Series on Languages and Linguistics* No. 21, pp. 113–22.
[2] Cf. G. Nickel and K. H. Wagner, 'Contrastive linguistics and language teaching', p. 248, n. 18.

question of whether interference phenomena depend in some ways on the particular level of language concerned must also be investigated by the psychology of learning.[1]

Contrastive linguistics has shown the necessity for a differentiation of teaching material. Financial considerations, however, will impose limitations on such a differentiation. Most foreign-language teachers in Germany know that the problems of teaching foreign languages vary in character according to the dialect area (the North vs. the South, etc.). Nevertheless, separate textbooks for each dialect region will not appear reasonable since on the one hand there are on the whole more correspondences than differences in these areas and on the other hand the cost of textbooks would be increased unnecessarily. However, in the case of 'the foreign learner' it should at least be possible to produce textbooks adapted for teaching learners speaking related languages. The groups of related languages could be more exactly defined with the aid of contrastive analyses.

At all events, contrastive linguistics can provide us with a clearer conception of common and divergent features of different languages providing it makes use of suitable models for description.[2] Perhaps contrastive analysis can also show us a new and more systematic approach to the question of universals. Although it is still in its infancy, it has already made valuable contributions in the field of foreign-language teaching, where, however, it should be considered as only one of several currents in a deep ocean.

---

[1] For an attempt to distinguish between difficulties on different linguistic levels cf. L. Dušková, 'On sources of errors in foreign language learning'. For phonological differences and difficulties cf. B. Malmberg, *Le rôle des universités dans la formation des professeurs de langues*. Council of Europe Project 50/5 (mimeographed version, 1969), pp. 60 ff. and p. 77. Also B. Malmberg, 'Probleme der Ausspracheschulung', *Zielsprache Deutsch*, Heft 1, 1. Jahrgang (1970), pp. 2–12.

[2] Cf. R. J. Di Pietro, *Methods in Contrastive Linguistics* (forthcoming).

A stratificational approach to contrastive analysis

ROGER L. SNOOK

---

1   *The objectives of contrastive analysis*

Despite wide agreement that the ultimate objective of pedagogically orientated contrastive analysis is the improvement of foreign-language teaching, one rarely finds in the literature explicit statements on how cross-linguistic comparison may be expected to achieve this aim. Perhaps the most frequent assumption is that by contrasting SL and TL structures one will be able to predict learners' TL errors and in some way adapt teaching materials to take account of the errors. This conception is surely based on a false premiss, for it is by no means intuitively plain that mere scrutiny and comparison of SL and TL structures will permit the prediction of TL deviations: non-isomorphism between SL and TL structures, and points of relatively greater structural complexity in the TL, for instance, are not correlated *a priori* with TL-learners' errors. This is not, however, to deny the possibility of establishing regular correlations between TL errors on the one hand and relations of similarity and dissimilarity between SL and TL structures on the other. But in order to do so one must first know what kinds of error are made. When a sufficiently large corpus of errors is available and the corresponding areas of structure in the SL and TL have been analysed, one may hope to establish what kinds of interlingual discrepancy are potentially associated with certain TL errors. The analysis will most likely proceed from a taxonomy of error-associated structural contrasts to explanatory hypotheses and will aim at a general theory of error genesis for the SL and TL concerned. An ultimate goal of such research would be a universal theory of error genesis for any SL and TL. A comprehensive theory of error genesis will also attempt to explain why certain errors rather than others occur in given TL idiolects[1]

---

[1] A TL idiolect is an individual foreign learner's current approximation to the native speaker's language system.

and why some TL idiolects are error free at certain structure points while others are not. In accounting for such individual differences the linguistic theory of error genesis will no doubt have to be integrated into a general theory of learning. An important complement to error analysis in setting up a theory of error genesis will be the investigation of points in SL and TL structure not associated with TL errors.

Explanation of TL errors, then, not their prediction, is a main objective of contrastive analysis.[1] There is, however, a further justification for contrastive analysis: the establishment of cross-linguistic semological equivalents for the purpose of teaching meaning or content structure. Where areas of the conceptual systems underlying the SL and the TL are isomorphous, meanings can probably be taught most effectively by pointing to semological equivalences between the SL and TL. Thus the most convenient way of teaching one of the meanings of *also* to German learners is to point to the equivalent meaning of *auch*. If instruction is exclusively in the TL, the teacher has to confront the learner with a series of instances of *also* in context in the hope that the learner will create the association between the TL lexeme and the SL meaning on his own accord. Often this procedure makes too great demands on the learner; at all events it is time-wasting and pointless unless instruction making use of the SL is impracticable. The method of teaching meaning by explanation in the TL is frequently ineffectual even with advanced learners, largely because we lack a metalanguage for discourse on the conceptual elements and structures involved. This is particularly evident when the lexemes whose meanings are to be taught are so-called 'logical' words or formators. How, for instance, does one explain in English the meaning of such lexemes as *also, nevertheless, in case, until, at all events, in order that* other than by adducing synonyms, where available, which may, of course, also be unknown to the foreign learner? In this context it is pertinent to observe that L_1 and L_2 learning are very different processes. L_1 learning is largely coincident with the process of concept formation and to some extent conditions the latter. By the time L_2 acquisition begins the learner has built up a complex system of concepts. These concepts do not have to be relearnt during L_2 acquisition; they have in the main to be connected up to grammatical and lexical forms of the L_2. Since the semologies of different languages are not isomorphous at all points, a certain amount of regrouping of conceptual

---

[1] Similar views have been expressed, for instance, by Mackey (1966: 200 f.), Lee (1968: 188 ff.) and Catford (1968: 160). My argument is that error prediction is not only in most cases unnecessary, but also unfeasible without prior error analysis which has led to generalizations on error genesis. This argument is stated rather more fully in Snook (1969).

elements already acquired will be necessary to fit them into semological categories of the L_2; but many of the basic semological elements (sememes in stratificational terminology) seem to be common to a large number of languages. A further important function of contrastive analysis, then, is to facilitate the teaching of meaning by displaying equivalences in the semologies of the SL and TL.

2 The non-relevance of transformational generative models for CA

Perhaps most linguists will agree that explicitly formulated models of language are of heuristic value in linguistic research. As uncommitted observers of linguistic theorizing know, models in linguistics have a way of acquiring a life of their own and of flying off into conceptual space beyond the control of their creators. Overenthusiasm for formalization may lead one to shirk the task of accounting for the data of language behaviour and result in trivia. However, good models can engender good research and they would seem to be as useful in applied linguistics as they are in other empirical sciences.

In recent years much enthusiasm has been generated among contrastivists by N. Chomsky's transformational model.[1] Transformational and stratificational grammars are mutually exclusive generative models of language. Before examining the potentialities of stratificational models for contrastive analysis, let us briefly discuss, then, the relevance of transformational generative grammar for pedagogically orientated linguistics. First, we may observe that language learning in general and such aberrations in language behaviour as TL errors are psychological processes or result from such processes. It follows that a theory which attempts to account for these phenomena should be couched in psychological terms or be relatable in an explicit way to the psycholinguistic data. Does the transformational model fulfil these conditions? This depends on whether the generating processes of Chomsky-type formal grammars can be regarded as describing, or as being systematically related to the psychological processes by which people actually produce and recognize sentences.

---

[1] Few critics of 'applied transformational grammar' will wish to deny that many publications on CA written from the transformational viewpoint contain valuable insights into language structure and behaviour; although some will maintain that these insights have been achieved incidentally or despite the theoretical framework used. The remarks made in section 2 have, of course, no bearing on the question of the adequacy of TG as a formal system; nor should they be construed as implying criticism of non-pedagogically orientated cross-linguistic comparisons based on the transformational model. It must in fairness be added that leading transformationalists have not generally advocated 'applied transformational grammar'.

In the early 1960s G. A. Miller and other psychologists who had been influenced by Chomsky's work carried out a series of psycholinguistic experiments, involving matching and recall tasks, to test the hypothesis that certain operations whereby transformational grammars generate structural descriptions, in particular transformations themselves, have psychological reality. These well-known experiments are summarized and interpreted by the MIT scholars Fodor and Garrett (1966). Experiments involving passive, negative, interrogative and emphatic transformations appeared to confirm the hypothesis that derivational history predicts performance complexity. However, as Fodor and Garrett (1966: 148) and Sutherland (1966: 159 f.) point out, certain variables (sentence length, meaning, frequency of usage) were not taken into account in these investigations; hence the experiments do not provide strong support for the thesis that language behaviour mechanisms are closely related to the Chomskyan model. In further experiments dealing with auxiliary expansion, the comparative construction and particle and adverb movement results were negative: it was found that performance measures of sentence complexity do not clearly correlate with derivational history. In the light of these findings Fodor and Garrett conclude: 'The problem may not be that our experimental procedures fail to measure perceptual complexity, but rather that it is a mistake to claim psychological reality for the operations whereby grammars generate structural descriptions.' (Fodor and Garrett, 1966: 152.)[1]

This conclusion seems to accord with Chomsky's own view: 'To avoid what has been a continuing misunderstanding, it is perhaps worthwhile to reiterate that a generative grammar is not a model for a speaker or a hearer... When we say that a sentence has a certain derivation with respect to a particular generative grammar, we say nothing about how the speaker or hearer might proceed, in some practical or efficient way, to construct such a derivation. These questions belong to the theory of language use – the theory of performance' (Chomsky 1965: 9).

We may sum up the argument of the preceding paragraphs by saying that the transformational generative model is a model of linguistic *competence*, i.e. an axiomatic representation (one among several possible ones) of the linguistic information which an ideal speaker-hearer may be regarded as having at his disposal; it does not lay claim to being a model of the

---

[1] It is true that most of the psycholinguistic experiments referred to were based on the early version of Chomsky's model. This has, of course, been meanwhile extensively revised by Chomsky (1965) and others. Since, however, the transformational operations involved are regarded as similar in both versions of the theory, the findings of the Chomskyan psycholinguists still appear relevant to the later version of the model.

mechanism underlying a speaker-hearer's verbal *performance*. In view of these considerations it is difficult to see what role transformational generative grammar can play in applied linguistics, and more especially in pedagogically orientated contrastive analysis.

3 *Stratificational models as performance models*

A generative model of language which does attempt to account for the behavioural processes underlying language production and perception, and which, therefore, is potentially utilizable in pedagogically orientated linguistics, is Sydney Lamb's stratificational grammar (SG). This model, which originated with Lamb in the early 1960s and which has subsequently been developed by Lamb himself, H. A. Gleason, P. R. Reich and other North American scholars, not only claims for its structural descriptions the explicitness of transformational generative treatments together with the merit of greater theoretical parsimony: it also specifically incorporates performance axioms into the theory in order to satisfy conditions of behavioural as well as linguistic adequacy. It may be regarded, therefore, as a combined competence and performance model.[1]

Stratificational theory views language as a device for converting or recoding information from one form into another. Discourse production consists of a transduction process, taking place in real time, between content (conceptual structure) and expression (speech sounds, graphic marks). Speech comprehension involves a similar transduction process within the same device, but in the opposite direction, from expression to content. The system underlying language behaviour is formalized as a finite network of relationships or logical elements. The various kinds of mutation rule of transformational theory are replaced in Lamb's SG by the conception of impulses or signals passing through the network of linguistic relationships. Reich (1968*a*, 1969; cf. also 1968*b*, 1968*c*, 1968*d*) is exploring the

---

[1] The most comprehensive work to date on SG is Lamb (1966*b*). Lamb, however, regards this as an interim document and has introduced some theoretical modifications since 1966. Numerous articles on SG have appeared in various journals since the mid-1960s. A collection of basic stratificational writings, some hitherto unpublished, will appear in Makkai and Lockwood (forthcoming). An annotated bibliography of publications on SG up to 1968 is given in Fleming (1969). Perhaps the best way into SG is first to read Gleason (1964), and then Lamb (1966*b*) in conjunction with Bennett (1968), who briefly explains some recent innovations in theory. A fairly non-technical account of stratificational semology and lexicology which takes account of post-1966 modifications is Lamb (1969). For the general theoretical and historical background of SG, with particular reference to Hjelmslev, see Lamb (1966*a*). Applications of SG in contrastive discourse structure analysis are discussed in Gleason (1968). Gleason's stratificational model differs in some respects from Lamb's.

possibility of building into the network neurophysiologically motivated restrictions intended to make it behave consistently with the way the brain is believed to function. Reich hypothesizes that the relational network underlying language behaviour consists of behaviourly defined finite-state devices which intercommunicate by using small sets of discrete signals moving through the network in parallel, asynchronously and in real time. Certain aspects of this model are being tested with the Relational Network Simulator (cf. Reich 1968b) in connection with the Linguistic Automation Project at Yale University.

As Reich himself points out, the relational network approach within SG 'must stand or fall entirely on its ability to handle linguistic and psycholinguistic data' (Reich 1968a: 15).

I do not wish to suggest, therefore, that SG in its present form is a ready-built performance model adapted to all the needs of applied linguistic research. However, I do think it is clear that an otherwise adequate model which attempts to incorporate performance axioms from the start will be more useful in pedagogically orientated linguistic research than one which does not. I believe that the following are among the most fruitful insights SG has to offer pedagogically orientated contrastive analysis:

(1) The notion that linguistic encoding and decoding operations take place in real time. This condition finds no place in transformational generative grammar, yet it is essential for a behavioural model of language.

(2) The conception that discourse generation is under content control, i.e. that operations of information transduction which result in expression output are predetermined at the content end of language.

(3) The assumption that a language comprises several sub-codes or strata, each with a separate tactics (syntax) which generates well-formed combinations at that level.

(4) The conception that when there is alternation between linguistic elements, the alternants are realizations of a concurrently existing, higher-level entity, and that when there is contextual conditioning of the alternants (i.e. when they are not in free variation) this conditioning occurs at a higher level than that on which the realizations exist and is prior in time to the latter.

(5) The supposition that encoding and decoding may be accounted for by the same linguistic mechanism. This enables the model to be used in research on errors in receptive control.

(6) The view that a semology (that part of a language which models content or meaning structure) is as important an element of the language system as grammar or phonology.

I shall now proceed to sketch the mechanism of Lamb's model as a preliminary to exemplifying how two problems of English–German contrastive analysis can be approached within a stratificational framework.

4 The mechanism of stratificational grammar

A language is regarded as consisting of a system of relationships. The totality of relationships linking content and expression is termed the *realizational chain*. Relationships comprising the realizational chain are *realizational relationships*. Within the realizational chain a few basic types of relationship are found, and these appear in certain recurring configurations called *patterns*. Patterns in turn are present in recurring configurations known as *strata*. In Lamb's 1966 version of SG six strata are recognized for English. The stratum contiguous to content is termed the *hypersememic* stratum; then, moving downwards towards expression (content is conventionally placed at the top, expression at the bottom of diagrams) we have consecutively the *sememic, lexemic, morphemic, phonemic and hypophonemic* strata. The two upper strata can be called the *semology*, the two central ones the *grammar*, and the two lower ones the *phonology* of the language. Recent research in stratificational grammar suggests that the model can be simplified by collapsing the hypersememic and sememic strata into a single semological stratum and the phonemic and hypophonemic strata into one phonological stratum (see Lamb 1969 *a*, *b*, 1970: 9 ff., cf. also Reich 1968 *d*: 22).

Associated with each stratum, but lying outside the realization chain is a set of relations which provides during encoding for the temporal ordering of realizational relationships and for the choice between alternate realizations at that point of the realizational chain. This set of relationships is known as the *tactics* or syntax of the stratum. There is one tactics for each stratum.

Relationships in the realizational chain and in the various tactic systems are built up of three *fundamental dichotomies*: (1) conjunction: disjunction, (2) unordered: ordered, (3) downward: upward. The six elements of the fundamental dichotomies may be regarded as the 'atoms' of linguistic structure. They occur in a few combinations which may be looked on as the 'molecules' of language. Language structure is described by Lamb and his followers in terms of two-dimensional graphs made up of *nodes* standing for various combinations of elements in the fundamental dichotomies and of *lines* which connect up the nodes.[1] Discourse production and reception

---

[1] An algebraic notation is also used in SG. The graphic notation, however, is held to provide a more direct portrayal of structural relationships and is thus the preferred notation with Lamb and his followers.

is interpreted dynamically in terms of impulses or signals passing through the network of lines and nodes. In the encoding process impulses pass *downward* from the content end (semology) by way of the grammar to the expression end (phonology); in decoding they move *upward* from the expression end to the content end.

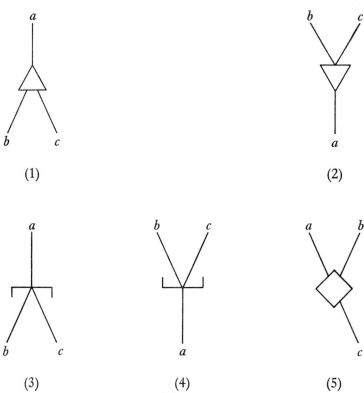

FIG. I. Some common types of node

Fig. I shows six common types of node. The names and dynamic interpretation of the illustrated nodes are as follows:[1]

(1) *Downward ordered* AND. In encoding, an impulse passes down line *a*, then down *b*, and only then down *c*. The ordering of impulses through *b* and *c* is a temporal one. In decoding, an impulse travels up *b*, and only then up *c* and *a*.

(2) *Upward unordered* AND. Encoding: Impulses pass down *b* and *c*, not necessarily simultaneously; when both impulses have arrived at the node,

[1] Diamond nodes were introduced after the appearance of Lamb (1966b); they are explained in Lamb (1969: 19 ff.). More than two lines may be connected to the plural side of a node.

and only then, an impulse moves down *a*. Decoding: An impulse from *a* moves up *b* and *c* simultaneously.

(3) *Downward unordered* OR. Encoding: An impulse travels down *a* and then passes on through lower nodes either via *b* or via *c*. The disjunction is exclusive. Decoding: An impulse passes up *b* or up *c* and then on through *a*.

(4) *Upward unordered* OR. Encoding: Either *b* or *c* is activated before *a* is. The disjunction is also exclusive. Decoding: *a* is first activated, and then either *b* or *c*.

(5) *Diamond node*. These nodes are at the points of intersection between the realizational chain and the several tactic systems. Encoding: An impulse passes first down *a* from higher up in the realizational chain; then an impulse comes in from the tactics of the stratum; then, when the impulses from *a* and *b* have reached the node, an impulse moves down *c*. Decoding: An impulse comes up *c* from lower in the realizational chain; then an impulse comes in from the tactics; finally an impulse travels to higher in the realizational chain via *a*.

According to Lamb there are no 'items' or 'abstract objects' within linguistic structure such as have been postulated in the Boas–Sapir–Bloomfield–Harris–Chomsky tradition; language consists entirely of inter-connected relationships (cf. Lamb 1966*b*: 40, 1969*b*: 10 ff.; Lockwood 1970: 14 ff.). However, it is found convenient for purposes of exposition to use labels, some of them similar to those of conventional structural linguistics and transformational grammar, in order to designate certain points of structural relevance within the network of relationships. Points in the network which are connected directly to the tactics, i.e. the diamond nodes, are given the suffix *-eme*; thus we have, according to the stratum, *sememes, lexemes, morphemes, phonemes* (and in the 1966 system also *hyper-sememes* and *hypophonemes*). An AND node in the realizational chain is termed a *sign* (*sememic sign, lexemic sign*, etc.).[1] Lines at the bottom of a stratum which lead to the *-emes* of the stratum below are given the suffix *-on* (*semon, lexon*, etc.). The use of such labels is illustrated in Fig. 2.

Important types of realizational relationship are:

(1) *Composite realization* (CR). This is the relation involved when a line

---

[1] Lines which lead directly into *-ons* at the bottom of a stratum are also referred to as signs. Symbols for *-emes*, signs and *-ons* are placed within oblique strokes and preceded by capitals which identify the type of structural point and the stratum on which the latter is located; e.g. S = sememe, SS = sememic sign, SN = semon, L = lexeme, etc. Sememic elements are here identified by listing their principal lexemic realizations within the oblique strokes. Lexemic elements are symbolized by their conventional graphemic realizations. In a fuller treatment of English and German structure a more specific symbolization would have to be used for lexemic elements in order to distinguish lexemes with similar graphemic realizations.

leads downwards from an -*eme* via a sign (a downward AND) to a combination of -*ons*. For instance, on the lexemic stratum we have an adverbial lexeme ᴸ/as well/, as in *Frank came as well*, which is a complex lexeme made up of the lexons ᴸᴺ/as/ and ᴸᴺ/well/, each of which is connected up with several other lexemes (cf. *Jack is as big as John*; *well-being*; *She is not feeling well*). Fig. 2. illustrates the composite realization of ᴸ/as well/.

(2) *Portmanteau realization* (PR). In this case two or more -*emes* are connected to an upward AND situated below them in the realizational chain. In English semology there are lines running downward from the sememe ˢ/negation/ and from the sememe which is realized on the lexemic stratum as the lexemes ᴸ/also/, ᴸ/as well/, etc. into an upward AND. The latter is a sememic sign which has on the lexemic stratum the alternating realizations ᴸᴺ/nor/ and ᴸᴺ/neither/ (see Fig. 2).

(3) *Neutralization* (N). Lines run down from two or more -*emes* to an upward OR or from two or more -*ons* to an upward OR above an individual -*eme*. For instance, in English there are two lexemes each with connections leading down to an upward OR, the lower line from which runs to the lexon ᴸᴺ/too/; cf. *I am coming too* and *It is too hot*. (We postulate two lexemes because each *too* exhibits a different kind of lexotactic behaviour.)

(4) *Diversification* (D). Several connections run downward from a downward OR, either to -*emes*, or to signs or -*ons*. For instance, the lexons ᴸᴺ/nor/ and ᴸᴺ/neither/, when they each realize the meaning 'negation' together with the meaning 'also' (portmanteau realization), are in free variation as alternate realizations of a lexeme ᴸ/nor-neither/ (see Fig. 2). We postulate a single lexeme as the realizate of the two lexons because in this function *nor* and *neither* exhibit the same lexotactic behaviour.

The area of a stratum which contains the -*ons* and signs is termed the *sign pattern*. Between the sign pattern, at the bottom of the stratum, and the -*emes* is an area with downward ORs, each of which indicates that an -*eme* has one or more free variants as realizations (signs or -*ons*; the relationship is diversification): this area is known as the *lower alternation pattern*. The area containing the -*emes* is called the *knot pattern* or *diamond pattern*. Above the knot pattern, at the top of the stratum, is an area containing downward ORs, which indicate that an -*on* of the next higher stratum has alternate -*emic* realizations (relationship: diversification), and upward ORs, which signify that several -*ons* of the next higher stratum have a single -*emic* realization (relationship: neutralization): this area is the *upper alternation pattern* of the stratum. The tactics of the stratum is conventionally regarded as lying to the right of the knot pattern.

5   The realization of ᔆ/*also-as well-too-either*/ in English and German

This and the following analysis have been greatly oversimplified for purposes of exposition. The intention is simply to indicate how problems of contrastive analysis may be approached within a stratificational framework. I shall treat briefly two very frequent kinds of encoding error made by advanced German-speaking learners of English. Using a stratificational framework for our contrastive analysis, we shall be particularly interested in seeing whether errors can be classified in terms of the realizational relationships and patterns involved. It will also be of interest to establish whether a taxonomy of errors can be set up which relates the variables persistency and frequency of error to location on a particular stratum, to a particular stratal pattern, and to type of realizational relationship involved. These points can only be touched on in this paper.

Sentences (1) to (7) exemplify common advanced learners' errors involving the lexemes ᴸ/*also*/, ᴸ/*as well*/, ᴸ/*too*/ and ᴸ/*either*/:

(1) He has *as well* seen the *Victory*.	TE
(2) He has seen *too* the *Victory*.	TE
(3) He has seen *also* the *Victory*.	TE
(4) He has *also* not seen the *Victory*.	RE
(5) He *too* has not seen the *Victory*.	RE
(6) He has not seen *either* the *Victory*.	TE
(7) *Also* today you can go over Nelson's flagship.	TE + RE

(The letters on the right will be explained below.)

If we compare the SL and TL networks involved, we see that on the lexemic stratum English displays far more complex structuring than German, whereas on the sememic stratum English is only slightly more complex (we shall not take the analysis down to the morphemic stratum since the errors concerned are not generated at this level). Fig. 2 shows the part of the English realizational chain involved. Diversification (cf. the downward OR) is exhibited above the lexemes: that is to say, they are all realizations of the same semon ˢᴺ/*also-as well-too-either*/. This semon stands in a one-to-one relationship with a sememe above it and the latter stands in a one-to-one relationship with the concept of 'also-ness'. It will be noted that in the dialect represented here the lexemic signs ᴸˢ/*also*/, ᴸˢ/*as well*/, ᴸˢ/*too*/, ᴸˢ/*either*/ are not in free variation: if they were, i.e. if they displayed equivalent lexemic distribution, the diversification would be in the lower lexemic alternation pattern instead of in the upper one (cf. section 4). Separate lexemes are posited as realizates for these lexemic signs

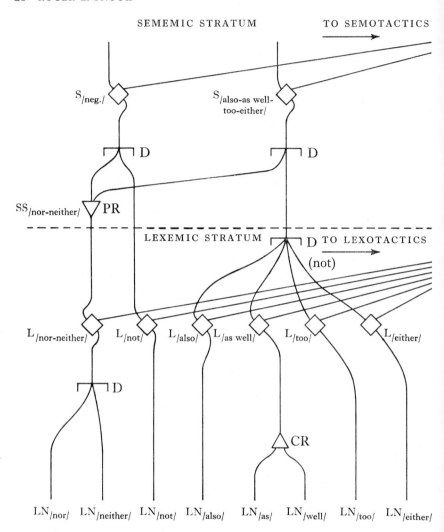

FIG. 2. Part of sememic and lexemic strata of one kind of British
English (simplified). (not) = condition on L/either/

because none of the forms shares all its possible lexemic environments with
any of the others – although each shares *some* environments with the others.

The lexeme L/either/ differs in an important way from the other three:
there is a condition on its occurrence not shared by the others. L/either/
occurs as the realization of S/also-as well-too-either/ when the latter co-
occurs (on the sememic stratum, of course) with the sememe S/negation/.
The lexotactics is context-sensitive and only permits L/either/ under these

circumstances. (There are, it is true, some English dialects and idiolects which allow the realization of ᴸ/also/ when ˢ/negation/ is activated.) Here the sememe ˢ/negation/ is realized as the lexeme ᴸ/not/. We say *I am also going* or *I am going too/as well*, but *I am not going either*. Lexemes ᴸ/also/, ᴸ/as well/, ᴸ/too/ and ᴸ/either/ may be regarded as synonymous since they are all realizations of the same sememe and, consequently, of the same element of cognitive meaning. They may also be considered interlingually synonymous with the German lexemes ᴸ/auch/ and ᴸ/ebenfalls/: the semological structures underlying the lexemes are interlingually isomorphous. Fig. 2 also shows that an alternative to the combination ᴸ/not/ + ᴸ/neither/ exists in English: the lexeme ᴸ/nor-neither/, which may be realized either by lexemic sign ᴸˢ/nor/ or by ᴸˢ/neither/ (cf. section 4).

The following are corrected versions of sentences (1) to (7):

(8) He has seen the *Victory as well.*   (1)

(9) He has seen the *Victory too.*   (2)

(10a) He has *also* seen the *Victory.*   (3)

(10b) He has seen the *Victory also.*   (3)

(11) He has not seen the *Victory either.*   (4, 5, 6)

(12a) Today you can *still* go over Nelson's flagship.   (7)

(12b) You can *still* go over Nelson's flagship today.   (7)

(Numbers on the right refer to the incorrect sentences on p. 27.)

The errors in sentences (1) to (7) fall into three categories:

(1) *Tactic errors* (TEs). These are said to occur when the tactics of a stratum has generated ill-formed combinations of stratificational *-emes*, as is the case with the sentences marked TE.

(2) *Realizational errors* (REs). These fall into several subcategories according to the realizational relationship involved. In the examples listed only diversification is concerned: if ᴸ/also/ or ᴸ/too/ or ᴸ/as well/ is realized when ˢ/negation/ has been activated, a wrong line from the downward OR has been chosen and an RE results. The same would apply if the 'marked' form ᴸ/either/ were realized in the absence of an activated ˢ/negation/, as in *I am going either*; but this error does not seem to occur in actual TL idiolects. (Strictly speaking, the kind of aberration I am calling 'realizational error' is in reality also a tactic error since the selection among alternant contextually conditioned realizations is determined by the tactics of the stratum; but the terminological distinction is convenient.)

(3) *Combined tactic and realizational errors* (TE + RE). Ill-formed tactic combinations occur simultaneously with wrong selection of alternant realizations or with other REs.

Let us now contrast the relevant area of the realizational chain of English with the corresponding network of German. German is very simple here (see Fig. 3). Sememic structure is isomorphous with that of English except that there is no portmanteau realization of the sememes ^{S}/Negation/ and ^{S}/auch-ebenfalls/. Where English has four lexemes below the downward OR, German has only two, *viz.* ^{L}/auch/ and ^{L}/ebenfalls/, the latter being complex. Neither alternant is contextually conditioned by ^{S}/Negation/. German is less redundant than English at this structure point, but has less scope for stylistic variation. The tactics of English and German are here of about equal complexity. Sentences ($13a$) and ($13b$) render (8), (9), ($10a$), ($10b$); (14) renders (11); ($15a$) and ($15b$) render ($12a$) and ($12b$).

($13a$) Er hat *auch* die *Victory* gesehen.

($13b$) Er hat die *Victory auch* gesehen.

(14) Er hat die *Victory auch* nicht gesehen.

($15a$) *Auch* heute (noch) kann man Nelsons Flaggschiff besichtigen.

($15b$) Man kann Nelsons Flaggschiff *auch* heute noch besichtigen.

(Differences in meaning brought about by manipulating suprasegmentals are not considered in this brief treatment.)

In the light of the errors in (1) to (7) and the structural comparisons, we might draw the fairly obvious conclusion that TL tactic errors occur where SL and TL tactic patterns differ or where tactic arrangements of the SL do not occur in the TL, and vice versa. It was pointed out that German has no portmanteau corresponding to English ^{SS}/nor-neither/. From the further observation that German speakers' English TL idiolects frequently do not make use of the English portmanteau (*I am not either* or *I am also not* are very much more common than *Nor am I*), one might tentatively infer that the absence of a sememic portmanteau in the SL corresponding to one in the TL inhibits the laying down of this structure in learning the TL or in some way interferes with its activation if it has been laid down. One might also set up the tentative hypothesis that where the TL exhibits diversification in the upper lexemic alternation pattern, with the alternants being conditioned, and the SL has at the corresponding structure point no diversification or has diversification with free variation of the alternants, then TL errors may occur which consist in the failure to realize one of the conditioned -*emic* forms of the TL. The latter hypothesis receives some support from the following example.

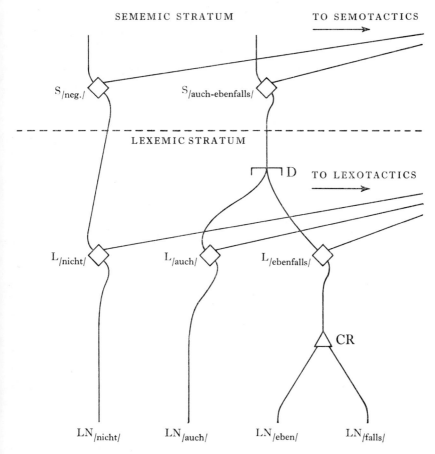

SEMEMIC STRATUM   TO SEMOTACTICS

LEXEMIC STRATUM

TO LEXOTACTICS

FIG. 3. Part of sememic and lexemic strata of standard German

6   The realization of SS/until-by/ in English and German

Considerably more difficult to analyse than the kind of mistake illustrated in section 5 are certain aberrations in semolexemic realization involving the lexemes L/until¹/ (preposition), L/until²/ (conjunction), L/by/, L/up to/, L/by the time that/. Examples are:

(16) Let me know *until* tomorrow.
(17) I shall have left *until* he gets here.
(18) What results have you obtained *until* now?
(19) We were not able to get there *until* Tuesday. (See below.)
(20) I shall stay *by* this evening.

These errors are all of the realizational type. In (16) the preposition ^{L}/by/ should have been used instead of ^{L}/until^1/. This substitution is extremely common and often persists in the TL idiolects of otherwise highly competent foreign speakers of English. A similar error is present in (17), only in this case the conjunction ^{L}/until^2/ has been wrongly substituted for the complex conjunction ^{L}/by the time (that)/. This error is not very common: Germans normally use an *already-when* construction here, e.g. *I shall already have left when he gets here*, this being modelled on the corresponding German lexemic construction. In (18) ^{L}/until^1/ has been incorrectly substituted for ^{L}/up to/; this is a very common mistake. Sentence (20) contains the converse of the error made in (16): ^{L}/by/ has been substituted for ^{L}/until^1/. This realization is very rare and perhaps only occurs under test conditions when both ^{L}/by/ and ^{L}/until^1/ have to be manipulated. Sentence (19) is lexically and sememically well-formed. However, if the proposition to be encoded implies that we were *not* at our destination at 6 o'clock, then (19) involves a realizational error.

The corrected sentences are:

(21)	Let me know *by* tomorrow.	(16)
(22)	I shall have left *by the time* he gets here.	(17)
(23)	What results have you obtained *up to* now?	(18)
(24)	We were not able to get there *by* Tuesday.	(19)
(25)	I shall stay *until* this evening.	(20)

German equivalents (there are some further possibilities) are:

(26)	Sagen Sie mir *bis* morgen Bescheid.	(21)
(27)	Ich werde *schon* weg sein, *wenn* er hier ankommt.	(22)
(28)	Welche Ergebnisse haben Sie *bis* jetzt erzielt?	(23)
(29)	Wir konnten *bis* Dienstag (*noch*) nicht dort sein.	(24)
(30)	Ich bleibe *bis* heute abend.	(25)

A thorough treatment of the problems involved here would entail a contrastive analysis of a fairly large area of English and German semology, including the realizates of such adverbial lexemes as ^{L}/already/, ^{L}/yet/, ^{L}/still/, ^{L}/schon/, ^{L}/noch/, and also aspectual features of various kinds. Such a treatment calls for a paper in itself, hence I shall confine myself to a brief discussion of the functions underlying *by*, *until* and *bis* exemplified by sentences (19), (21), (25), (26) and (30).

First, we may note that the *until* of (25) functions quite differently from the *until* of (19). If negated, sentence (25) gives:

(31) I shall not stay until this evening.

Sentence (19), however, although it also contains the lexemes ᴸ/not/+ᴸ/ until/ is not negative in the same sense as (25): it exhibits lexemic, but not sememic negation, whereas (25) is both lexemically and sememically negative. A sentence is lexemically negative when it contains a negative lexeme such as ᴸ/not/, ᴸ/nobody/, ᴸ/nothing/; it is sememically negative when it realizes the negation sememe. The ᴸ/not/ in (19) does not realize the ˢ/negation/. The *not...until* of (19) may, in fact, be regarded as a complex lexeme with discontinuous constituents which realizes a semon interlingually synonymous with the semon underlying the German lexeme ᴸ/erst/. The German equivalent of (19) is:

(32) Wir konnten *erst* Dienstag dort sein.

That (19) is not sememically negative is made clear by the fact that there is no corresponding positive sentence: we cannot say *We were able to get there until Tuesday*. Below the English -*on* in the upper lexemic alternation pattern is a downward OR since the alternate lexemic realization ᴸ/only/ is possible in some contexts. The alternant *not...until* is often absent in German TL idiolects: many Germans render (32) exclusively as *We could only be there on Tuesday*.

In the contexts under discussion, where German has *bis* English sometimes has *by*, sometimes *until*. Our problem here is to decide under what circumstances the forms *by* and *until* are realized. The problem can be stated in stratificational terms in the form of three hypotheses: (1) *By* and *until* are lexemic signs realizing a single lexeme; (2) they are alternating lexemes realizing the same sememic sign; (3) each is a separate lexeme realizing a separate sememic sign. In the case of *bis* we have to ascertain whether we have simple realization or neutralization between this form and the semology. Whether the sememic signs realized by *by*, *until* and *bis* are themselves simple realizations of single sememes (ultimate semological constituents) or portmanteau realizations of several sememes is not of great relevance for the present discussion. The first hypothesis can be discounted after a brief examination of the material. If *by* and *until* were lexemic signs they would always be interchangeable in a given sentence. This is clearly not the case, as is made evident by the TL errors. Like the first hypothesis, the second one assumes that *by* and *until* realize the same sememic sign, i.e. have the same cognitive meaning. The alternation between ᴸ/by/ and ᴸ/until/ would be accounted for by conditioning on the sememic stratum. This hypothesis does not at first sight seem very plausible in view of such apparent minimal pairs as *I need it by Friday* and *I need it until Friday*. The latter would seem to lend support to the third hypothesis, which posits a separate sememic sign, i.e. a different cognitive meaning, for each lexeme. However, a close analysis of the data appears to confirm the second hypothesis. What appear to some informants to be differences in meaning between ᴸ/by/ and ᴸ/until/ are most probably to be identified with semological elements in the environment of the underlying sign which condition the lexemic alternation. The sememic condition on the realization of ᴸ/until/ is a set of aspectual features which may be characterized by the term 'durative aspect'; the fairly complex set of aspectual features conditioning ᴸ/by/ may then be termed 'non-durative'. Both sets of aspectual features may be regarded as sememic signs. Neither conditioning factor is usually realized overtly on the lexemic stratum, although there is occasionally an adverbial lexicalization, as in *I need my car every day until the weekend.* The fact that *I need it by Friday* and *I need it until Friday* are not paraphrases may be accounted for by assuming that although ᴸ/by/ and ᴸ/until/ do not realize or 'express' the aspectual feature which conditions their alternation, they are able to *signal* this feature to the decoder owing to their habitual association with it.

German has a sememic sign ˢˢ/bis/, which can be regarded as interlingually synonymous with English ˢˢ/by-until/, and the relation between this sign and the lexemic realization ᴸ/bis/ is simple. This analysis, then, seems to give further support to the hypothesis that TL errors are likely to arise when the TL has semologically conditioned lexemic alternation corresponding to simple semolexemic realization in the SL.

7   Concluding remarks

From contrastive analyses I am carrying out on English and German the following general picture of error genesis seems to be emerging.

Most advanced German learners' errors are associated with the sememic and lexemic strata. Tactic errors are located mainly on the lexemic stratum, but ill-formed sememic combinations also occur, being frequently modelled on well-formed sememic combinations of German. These semotactic errors have not usually been recognized as such in the past and have often been given a pseudo-grammatical explanation.

The most persistent errors seem to involve semolexemic realizations. English is far more redundant in the area of semolexemic realization than German, whereas German is more redundant than English in the area of lexomorphemic realization. German is only superficially, i.e. lexomorphemically, a more complex language than English. Since English exhibits more complex semolexemic structuring than German and since this

A stratificational approach 35

structuring is largely 'invisible', English must probably be considered at least as difficult an L_2 as German.

As the examples in sections 5 and 6 suggest, serious difficulties are encountered by German learners where English exhibits semologically conditioned alternate lexemic realization and a corresponding diversification is not present in German. Even more persistent errors seem to arise when both languages have diversification at corresponding structure points, but with different conditions on the realizations. Errors do not appear frequent when English exhibits semolexemic neutralization where German has separate semolexemic realizations; on the contrary, this situation may facilitate learning. Persistent errors occur, however, when the situation is reversed, i.e. when separate realizations in English correspond to neutralization in German. This is the case with the German lexeme ᴸ/schon/, which apparently neutralizes semons for which there are in English perhaps six or more separate lexemic realizations.

Most persistent of all are errors which occur when English has separate semolexemic realizations combined with semologically conditioned alternations while German has neutralization at the corresponding structure point.

What is made particularly clear by the stratificational approach to contrastive analysis is, I think, the central role of semological comparison in this activity. The only kind of cross-linguistic comparison which can be made when content is not taken into account is the rather trivial one of comparing phonetic substance. Semological comparison is the keystone of contrastive analysis.

References

Alatis, J. E. (ed.) (1968). *Report of the Nineteenth Annual Round Table Meeting on Linguistics and Language Studies.* Monograph Series on Language and Linguistics No. 21. Washington D.C. (Georgetown University Press).
Bennett, D.C. (1968). 'English prepositions: a stratificational approach'. In *Journal of Linguistics* 4: 153–72.
Catford, J. C. (1968). 'Contrastive analysis and language teaching'. In Alatis (1968), pp. 159–73.
Chomsky, N. (1965). *Aspects of the Theory of Syntax*, Cambridge, Massachusetts, M.I.T. Press.
Fleming, I. (1969). 'Stratificational theory: an annotated bibliography'. In *Journal of English Linguistics* 3: 37–66.
Fodor, J. and Garrett, M. (1966). 'Some reflections on competence and performance'. In Lyons and Wales (1966), pp. 135–54.
Garvin, P. (ed.) (forthcoming). *Cognition: A Multiple View.*

Gleason, H. A. Jr. (1964). 'The organization of language: a stratificational view'. In Stuart (1964), pp. 75–95.

(1968). 'Contrastive analysis in discourse structure'. In Alatis (1968), pp. 39–63.

Hill, A. A. (ed.) (1969). *Linguistics Today*, New York, Basic Books.

Lamb, S. M. (1966a). 'Epilegomena to a theory of language'. In *Romance Philology* 19: 531–73.

(1966b). *Outline of Stratificational Grammar*, Washington, D.C., Georgetown University Press.

(1969a). 'Lexicology and semantics'. In Hill (1969), pp. 40–9.

(1969b). 'Linguistic and cognitive networks'. New Haven, Connecticut, Linguistic Automation Project, Yale University. To appear in Garvin (forthcoming).

Lee, W. R. (1968). 'Thoughts on contrastive linguistics in the context of language teaching'. In Alatis (1968), pp. 185–94.

Lockwood, D. G. (1970). '"Replacives" without process'. Mimeographed. To appear in Makkai and Lockwood (forthcoming).

Lyons, J. and Wales, R. J. (eds.) (1966). *Psycholinguistic Papers*, The Proceedings of the 1966 Edinburgh Conference. Edinburgh, Edinburgh University Press.

Makkai, V. B. (ed.) (forthcoming). *Phonological Theory: Evolution and Current Practice*. New York, Holt, Rinehart and Winston.

Makkai A. and Lockwood, D. G. (forthcoming). *Readings in Stratificational Linguistics*.

Mackey, W. F. (1966). 'Applied linguistics: its meaning and use'. In *English Language Teaching* 20: 197–206.

Reich, P. A. (1968a). 'Competence, performance, and relational networks'. New Haven, Connecticut, Linguistic Automation Project, Yale University.

(1968b). 'The relational network simulator'. New Haven, Connecticut, Linguistic Automation Project, Yale University.

(1968c). 'Symbols, relations, and structural complexity'. New Haven, Connecticut, Linguistic Automation Project, Yale University.

(1968d). 'The English auxiliaries: a relational network description'. New Haven, Connecticut, Linguistic Automation Project, Yale University.

(1969). 'The finiteness of natural language'. In *Language* 45: 831–43.

Snook, R. (1969). 'Welche Funktion hat die kontrastive Sprachwissenschaft?' Paper read at the Plenary Session of the GAL at Stuttgart, November 1969.

Stuart, C. J. J. N. (ed.) (1964). *Report on the Fifteenth Annual (First International) Round Table Meeting on Linguistics and Language Studies*. Monograph Series on Language and Linguistics, No. 17, Washington, D.C. Georgetown University Press.

Sutherland, N. S. (1966). Comments on Fodor and Garret (1966). In Lyons and Wales (1966), pp. 154–63.

Equivalence, congruence and deep structure

TOMASZ P. KRZESZOWSKI

In making comparisons of syntactic constructions in any two languages, at least two sorts of estimates must be made. First, it is necessary to find out which constructions in the two languages are comparable. Next it is necessary to see to what extent the compared constructions are formally similar.

It has been assumed that only those constructions which exhibit contextual equivalence are comparable (Halliday 1964: 115; Krzeszowski 1967). *Equivalent* constructions are those constructions which, at least sometimes, are mutually translatable. The relation which holds between such equivalents is called *textual equivalence* (Catford 1965: 27). In order to discover textual equivalents in a given context or situation one has to rely on the authority of a competent bilingual informant or translator (Halliday 1964: 115, Catford 1965: 27). The informant's judgments are based on his intuition, which underlies his linguistic competence in the two languages. Most investigators in the area of contrastive studies rely on their own competence and use themselves as informants, only occasionally referring to the judgments of other competent persons.

One of the aims of the present paper is to provide some insights into this kind of intuition and, in this way, to start the exploration of problems involved in the fundamental question: what accounts for the certainty of the bilingual informant (or translator) that particular constructions in two languages are or are not equivalent?

It is easy to see that equivalence is a notion intrinsically connected with the meaning of the compared constructions and that any approach to contrastive studies via the notion of equivalence is necessarily meaning-based.

Yet, when particular sentences are translated and their structures compared, it is also necessary to give an account of their form. Some of the equivalent constructions may consist of the same number of equivalent

[37]

formatives arranged in the same order. Such constructions have been referred to as *congruent* and the relation obtaining between them has been referred to as *congruence* (Krzeszowski 1967, Marton 1968).[1]

If we characterize various constructions in any two languages in terms of equivalence and formal correspondence, we shall observe that the sentences may be: (*a*) equivalent, formally different, (*b*) equivalent, formally similar – congruent, (*c*) non-equivalent, formally similar, (*d*) non-equivalent, formally different. The present paper will be mainly concerned with (*a*) and (*b*).

We shall work on the assumption that the first term in each pair refers to the deep structure of the compared constructions, while the second term refers to their surface structure. Moreover, we shall try to justify the following hypothesis: *equivalent constructions have identical deep structures even if on the surface they are markedly different.*[2] In this way we shall make a step towards explaining some of the translator's intuitions. Before we do this, however, we have to specify what we mean by the notion of 'deep structure'.

Lakoff (1968) derives a definition of deep structure from Katz and Postal (1964) and from Chomsky (1965). Deep structure is viewed as a level of linguistic analysis where (i) basic grammatical relations between fundamental grammatical categories are defined; (ii) selectional restrictions and co-occurrence relations are stated; (iii) appropriate grammatical categories receive lexical representations; (iv) inputs to transformational rules are provided.

Condition (ii) implies that the selectional restrictions and other co-occurrence relations stated at the level of deep structure make it possible to formulate correct generalizations about selectional restrictions and co-occurrence relations among the elements of the sentence.

Condition (iii) emerges from the assumption that the level of deep structure directly determines the semantic interpretation of the sentence. Since semantic interpretation involves semantic rules defined both in terms of semantic content of lexical items and by grammatical relations, conditions (ii) and (iii) are interdependent. Nevertheless, the semantic component as viewed by Katz *et al.* involves rules of a different order ('projection rules') than the rules of the Base.

This definition of deep structure renders it possible to make decisions as to the identity of deep structures of synonymous constructions which

---

[1] For a more elaborate discussion of congruence see Marton 1968.
[2] Cf. statements about universal base in Fillmore 1968, Bach 1968, and earlier about translation and meaning in Quine 1964.

are not identical on the surface. By demonstrating that the same selectional restrictions and other co-occurrence relations are in effect for synonymous but superficially different constructions, it is possible to infer that such constructions are essentially the same at the level of deep structure, where, in accordance with condition (ii) these restrictions are stated. In this way Lakoff is able to demonstrate the identity of deep structure of a pair of constructions represented by:

(1) Seymour sliced the salami with a knife

(2) Seymour used a knife to slice the salami

even though he is, as yet, unable to state what the deep structure of these constructions is, in terms of explicit rules.

Before we continue with our task, we shall make a preliminary step, trying to examine the syntactic behaviour of Polish equivalents of (1) and (2) to see whether the constructions which they represent are subject to a parallel set of co-occurrence restrictions. In this way we shall try to make sure that our initial hypothesis is not invalidated at the very outset.

Polish equivalents of (1) and (2) are:

(3) Seymour pokrajał salami nożem.

(4) Seymour użył noża aby pokrajać salami.[1]

In (3) the instrumental inflection with 'nożem' appears as a true equivalent of the preposition 'with' in (1) since the former, like the latter, has the purposive, instrumental sense (Lakoff 1968). Also in (4) the verb 'użyć' is a true equivalent of 'use' in (2) as both appear in the instrumental sense.

Let us represent the surface structures of the two pairs of sentences as:

(5) $NP_1 - V - NP_2 - with - NP_3$

(6) $NP_1 - use - NP_3 - to - V - NP_2$

(7) $NP_1 - V - NP_2 - inst - NP_3$

(8) $NP_1 - użyć \quad NP_3 - aby - V - NP_2$

where 'inst' in (7) stands for the instrumental inflection.

Lakoff has proved that the same set of selectional and co-occurrence restrictions holds in (5) and (6) and thus he has demonstrated the identity of the deep structures underlying these two constructions. It appears that a parallel set of restrictions applies with reference to (7) and (8):

I. In Polish as in English the verb represented by V must be characterized by the feature + Activity, for the sentence to be grammatical:

(9) a. Albert *computed* the answer with a sliderule.

    b. Albert used a sliderule to *compute* the answer.

---

[1] For brevity we ignore the question of aspect in Polish.

(10) a. Albert obliczył (uzyskał) odpowiedź suwakiem (even if 'na suwaku' sounds better).
  b. Albert użył suwaka aby obliczyć odpowiedź.

(11) a. *Albert *znał* odpowiedź suwakiem.
  b. *Albert użył suwaka aby *znać* odpowiedź.

II. Both in English and in Polish NP_1 must be animate:

(12) a. Peter hit Oliver with a hammer.
  b. Peter used a hammer to hit Oliver.

(13) a. Piotr uderzył Olivera młotkiem.
  b. Piotr użył młotka aby uderzyć Olivera.

(14) a. *Cios uderzył Olivera młotkiem.
  b. *Cios użył młotka aby uderzyć Olivera.

III. In none of the constructions can NP_2 have the same referent as NP_3:

(15) a. He unlocked the door with a master-key.
  b. He used a master-key to unlock the door.

(16) a. Otworzył drzwi wytrychem.
  b. Użył wytrycha aby otworzyć drzwi.

(17) a. *Otworzył drzwi nimi samymi.
  b. *Użył drzwi aby je otworzyć.

IV. In none of the constructions can NP_1 have the same referent as NP_3:

(18) a. Anatol broke the pane with the scared soldier.
  b. Anatol used the scared soldier to break the pane.

(19) a. Anatol wybił szybę przerażonym żołnierzem.
  b. Anatol użył przerażonego żołnierza aby wybić (nim) szybę.

(20) a. *?Anatol wybił soba szybę.
  b. *Anatol użył siebie aby wybić szybę.

V. Questions which are derived from (7) and (8) are both ambiguous in the same way as the equivalent questions in English:

(21) a. Did Seymour slice the salami with a knife?
  b. Did Seymour use a knife to slice the salami?

(22) a. Czy Seymour pokrajał salami nożem?
  b. Czy Seymour użył noża aby pokrajać salami?

All the four questions are ambiguous between at least two senses. First, they may be questions asking whether the action of slicing took place at all. Second, if the action is presupposed, they may ask for the confirmation of the information that the instrument used for the slicing of the salami was a knife.

VI. Negative constructions based on (7) and (8) are also ambiguous in the same way as the equivalent constructions in English:

(23) a. Seymour did not slice the salami with a knife.
b. Seymour did not use a knife to slice the salami.
(24) a. Seymour nie pokrajał salami nożem.
b. Seymour nie użył noża aby pokrajać salami.

All the four sentences may mean that the action of slicing did not take place, or, if the action is presupposed, that the instrument used was not a knife.

VII. In Polish as in English the verb phrase functioning as the complement of 'użyć' cannot be negated:

(25) a. *I used the knife not to slice the salami.
b. *I used the knife to not slice the salami.
(26) a. *Użyłem noża aby nie pokrajać salami.
b. *Użyłem noża nie aby pokrajać salami.

The fact that Polish equivalents of (5) and (6) are subject to a parallel set of selectional and co-occurrence restrictions opens hopeful vistas for empirical research to prove the hypothesis that equivalent constructions have identical deep structure.

In his paper Lakoff did not attempt to formulate any explicit rules representing relations between various grammatical categories in the deep structure. He contented himself with making some inferences about deep structure, the most significant one being that 'Deep structures must be somewhat more abstract (further removed from the surface) than previous research in transformational grammar has indicated' (Lakoff 1968). In the remainder of this paper we shall try to formulate some of the deep structure rules which account for the fact that (5), (6) and (7), (8) are equivalent.

Views on the nature of deep structure have recently changed towards the conviction that semantics is not interpretative but also generative and that, consequently, 'semantic representation and syntactic representation are of essentially the same formal nature' (McCawley 1968?).[1]

The formal apparatus used in this uniform representation is the general framework of symbolic logic or, more specifically predicate calculus where propositions correspond to deep structure sentences, functions correspond to verbs, and arguments to noun phrases or nouns.

We have no space for a detailed discussion of arguments in favour of such a conception of the Base accounting for the deep structures of

---

[1] For convincing arguments supporting this assertion see Lakoff and Ross 1967. For the defence of interpretative semantics see Chomsky 1968 and Katz 1970.

sentences. We have to confine ourselves to stating that the most satisfactory account of the Base conceived in logical terms as applied to natural languages has been suggested by Fillmore (1968). We shall adopt this framework, leaving theoretical discussions aside.[1]

It is assumed by Fillmore that the rules of the Base stated in terms of a modified predicate calculus are universal: 'In their deep structure the propositional nucleus of sentences in all languages consists of a V and one or more NPs, each having a separate case relationship to the P (and hence to the V).' Each proposition is preceded with Modality (M), so that the first rule of the universal base can be formulated as:

(27) $S \rightarrow M + P$ (Fillmore 1968)[2].

The proposition in (5), (6) and (7), (8) can be represented as follows:

(28) $P \rightarrow V + O + I + A$.[3]

The base representation of the four constructions before the insertion of lexical items is identical:

(29)

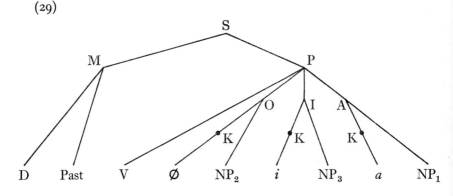

where D stands for Declarative Modality, i stands for the exponent of I on the surface – 'with' or 'use' in English, inflection of the instrumental case, 'przy pomocy + gen' or 'użyć + gen' in Polish; a stands for the exponents of A – 'by' and 'przez', respectively.

[1] There are many complications which for the purposes of this paper have to be ignored, e.g. the problem of whether or not NPs are derived in the Base from underlying sentences (see Bach 1968), the uncertain status of cases (relations?, categories? selection restrictions, see discussion in Robinson 1970 and Anderson forthcoming), and also lack of systematic criteria to decide whether a particular case is part of the proposition or whether it is derived from an embedded S. These and many other problems demand more research and cannot be dealt with in the present paper.

[2] Concerning sentence modality see Polański 1969.

[3] At the time of seeing this paper for print I am no longer convinced that I should be regarded as part of the same proposition along with O and A. For arguments against (28) see my *Prepositional Phrases in English* (forthcoming).

After the insertion of lexical items in place of Vs, NPs, and the exponents of the cases we obtain:

(30)

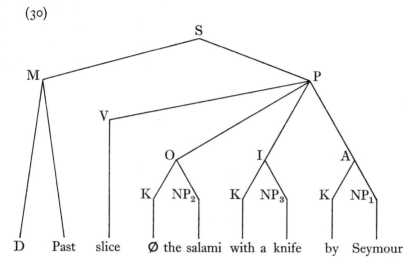

(31)

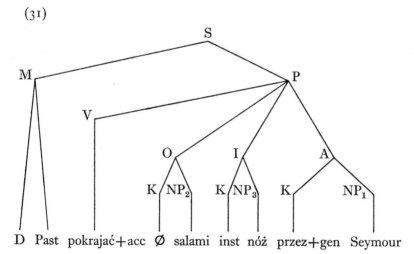

The deep structure of:

(2) Seymour used a knife to slice the salami.

and

(4) Seymour użył noża aby pokrajać salami.

is exactly the same as the deep structure of (1) and (3). In (2) and (4) 'use' and 'użyć' appear as exponents of I in place of 'with' and inst, respectively. It is worthy of note that even if 'nóż' in (4) appears on the surface with the genitive inflection it still represents the instrument involved in the process of slicing and in the deep structure is dominated by I. The genitive inflection in (4) is an idiosyncratic, surface characteristic of the Polish language where 'użyć' governs the genetive inflection which has nothing to do with the conceptual Instrumental dominating both NP_3s. Thus the deep structure of (2) and (4) can be represented as:

(32)

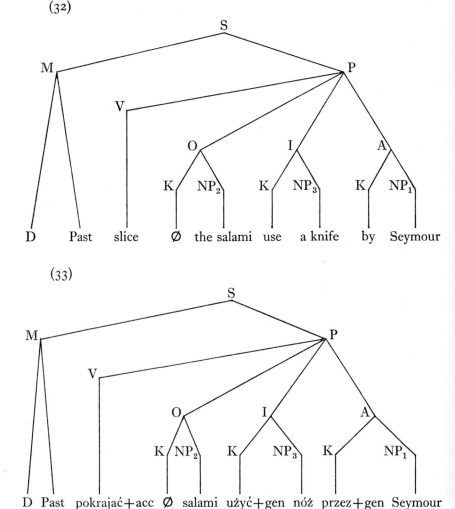

When A is subjectivized in (32) and (33), we obtain (34) and (35), respectively:

(34)

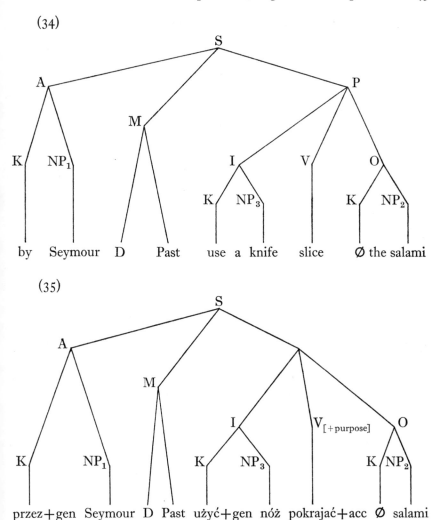

by   Seymour   D   Past   use   a   knife   slice   Ø the salami

(35)

przez+gen   Seymour   D   Past   użyć+gen   nóż   pokrajać+acc   Ø   salami

With the subjectivization of A in both (32) and (33) I is shifted in front of V according to a rule which I am unable to account for, at the moment. In addition, 'to' and 'aby' are inserted in front of the respective verbs. With the obligatory deletion of 'by' and 'przez + gen' and the necessary cosmetic transformations we eventually obtain:

(2) Seymour used a knife to slice the salami.

(4) Seymour użył noża aby pokrajać salami.

Even if the mechanism of the transformations remains somewhat obscure, it is obvious that the operations involved in the conversion of (32) to (34) and of (33) to (35) are exactly parallel and the resulting strings are nearly congruent. (They are not fully congruent because of the gen with 'nóż'.) When A in (30) becomes the subject, the preposition 'by' is deleted and after the necessary transformations we obtain:

(1) Seymour sliced the salami with a knife.

In Polish parallel operations yield:

(3) Seymour pokrajał salami nożem.

The subjectivization of O, both in English and in Polish, is only possible when the passive transformation is applied.[1]

The two processes account for the change of (30) to (36) and of (31) to (37):

(36)

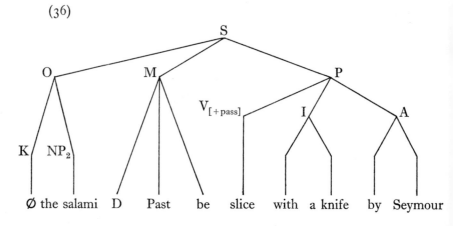

(37)

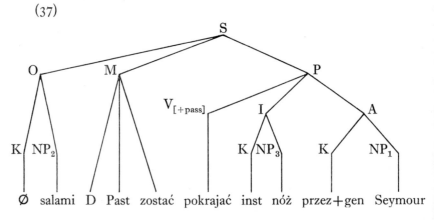

[1] Concerning the mechanism of the passive transformation, see Fillmore 1968: 37–40.

The resulting sentences are:

(38) The salami was sliced with a knife by Seymour.

(39) Salami zostało pokrajane nożem przez Seymoura.

I, too, may become the subject of the sentence. The subjectivization of I involves an interesting restriction, both in English and in Polish: the choice of the surface exponent of I is no longer a matter of free selection since 'use' and 'użyć' must be obligatorily inserted to represent I on the surface. In this case, too, the passive transformation must be obligatorily applied. The resulting sentences are:

(40) The knife was used by Seymour to slice the salami.

(41) Nóż został użyty przez Seymoura aby pokrajać salami.

I have tried to demonstrate the identity of deep structures of two English and Polish constructions involving the Instrumental case. This small bit of empirical evidence accords with Fillmore's and Bach's hypothesis that the Base is universal. Certainly, a great deal of research must be conducted before this hypothesis is granted the status of a full-fledged theory. In view of what has been said, intuitions of a bilingual informant involve the same fundamental operations as does paraphrase, since both involve the ability to associate particular sentences with the underlying deep structure or, in other words, ability to interpret the meaning of the sentences.

Differences between paraphrase and translation, which quite obviously exist, involve among other things, differences between various transformations through which the deep constructions work their way up to the surface. The study of this so far unexplored area deserves a separate and extensive treatment.

References

Anderson, John M. (forthcoming). *The Grammar of Case*, Cambridge University Press.

Bach, Emmon (1968). 'Nouns and noun phrases in universals'. In *Linguistic Theory* ed. Emmon Bach and Robert T. Harms, Holt, Rinehart and Winston, New York.

Catford, J. C. (1965). *A Linguistic Theory of Translation*, Oxford University Press, London.

Chomsky, Noam (1965). *Aspects of the Theory of Syntax*, M.I.T. Press, Cambridge, Mass.

 (1968). 'Deep structure, surface structure, and semantic interpretation' (xeroxed from the manuscript).

Fillmore, Charles, J. (1968). 'The case for case', in Bach and Harms.

Halliday, M. A. K., McIntosh, Angus and Strevens, Peter (1964). *The Linguistic Sciences and Language Teaching*, Longmans, London.

Katz, Jerrold J. (1970). 'Interpretative semantics and generative semantics', *Foundations of Language* 6, 2: 220–59.

Katz, Jerrold J., Postal, Paul M. (1964). *An Integrated Theory of Linguistic Descriptions*, Research Monograph No. 26, M.I.T. Press, Cambridge, Mass.

Krzeszowski, Tomasz P. (1967). 'Fundamental principles of structural contrastive studies', *Glottodidactica* II, 33–9.

Prepositional Phrases in English, in preparation.

Lakoff, George (1968) 'Instrumental adverbs and the concept of deep structure', *Foundations of Language* 4, 1: 4–29.

Lakoff, George and Ross, John R. (1967). 'Is deep structure necessary?' (duplicated).

McCawley, James. 'Meaning and the description of languages' (duplicated).

Marton, Waldemar (1968). 'Equivalence and congruence in transformational contrastive studies', *Studia Anglica Posnaniensia* I, 53–62.

Polanski, Kazimierz (1969), 'Sentence modality and verbal modality in generative grammar', *Biuletyn Fonograficzny* X, 91–100.

Robinson, Jane J. (1970). 'Case, category and configuration', *Journal of Linguistics* 6, 1: 57–80.

Quine, Willard V. (1964). *Meaning and Translation in the Structure of Language* ed. Jerry A. Fodor and Jerrold J. Katz, Prentice Hall, Englewood Cliffs, New Jersey.

What's so hard about that?

WILLIAM W. GAGE

This paper amplifies the not uncommon observation that, although a person already uses certain vocal noises at certain times, he may seem recalcitrant about producing similar noises in those situations appropriate for them in some language he is supposed to be learning.

A not overly significant example, but one I hope is sufficiently obvious to illustrate the concept intended, comes from the use of clicks in Southern Bantu languages. English speakers, at least all those I know well, already have clicks as part of their communicative repertoire. At the least, they use the one spelled 'tsk tsk'. But even those who readily say [ʖ] to horses do not readily transfer it to Xhosa. They seem to treat [ʖ] as though it were, so to speak, unfit for human consumption.

The description of my opening example could be quite concise, perhaps precisely because the sound is really not *in* English, but rather more sulking around the periphery of the speech community's customary practices.

Clearly within the language, however, we can find allophonic variants of sounds that are quite like some target sounds we might wish a learner to hit, but which still have a linguistic status such that rather than being able simply to have them carried over to a second language, we can only, as it were, dig them out.

For example, at the places where in the Trager–Smith transcription of English one writes a single bar, the normal situation is to have a slower than usual pace of the segmental material just before this 'juncture'. There is, though, at least for American English, another possible type of behavior at a phrase-break; in this latter case one cuts off the last syllable sharply, usually with a glottal stop. When the preceding segmental sound is a voiceless stop, the glottalization is normally simultaneous with it, as in:

²I'm ³síck³|? ³and ²tíred of it.[1]
³Nót³|? ³a ²bít.[1]

The sound at the end of *not* will, in such circumstances, be a 'glottalized' or 'ejective' [t'] – a suitable starting point for the type of [t'] required, say, for the Southern Sotho word *setulo*, 'chair'.

Much in the same vein, with the type of emphasis that serves as an English analogue of the French *accent d'insistance*, speakers of even northern U.S. dialects are quite prepared to come out with implosive voiced stops, but it is a considerable difficulty to get them to do it when they are not insisting.

A much more instructive example concerns the differences between the way pitch is used in English and in the contour-system tone languages of China and mainland Southeast Asia. In these languages the pitch phenomena associated with a given tone can be simulated to a degree that produces a passable imitation by using the expressive intonation associated with appropriate English monosyllabic utterances. Generally the similarity can be extended to include even the special modes of voice production associated with pitch as normal attributes of certain tones. Conversely, Southern Vietnamese tones, for example, as they are used on isolated syllables, would fit without too much of a wrench into American English utterances – provided these had the right expressive setting.

Thus the following Vietnamese syllables might serve for English phrases as indicated:

hão   ²Hów?!³ – mm – You may well ask.
xỏ   ¹Só,¹ I'm probably stuck with it.
nộ   ¹Nó,¹ I don't see any hope for it.
oanh   ³Óne,² two, three, four – they're coming out at the normal rate now.
áo   ⁴Ów!³ It hurt that time.

While it is quite true that the pitch sequences of a given sentence in a contour-system tone language are generally more complex than the intonational pitch changes in most English sentences, yet, an actor in an intense scene would often make just as many turns of pitch in just as short a time. So, in fact, on occasion, will the ordinary speaker when the variations mean something to him.

Southern Vietnamese tones present almost no inherent production problems for an American speaker; only on unstressed syllables can there be significant hearing problems. In spite of this, one can be faced with tremendous resistance of students to remembering the tone as part of words that are – otherwise – learned, and with an apparent reluctance to use the right pitch at the right time. What would seem to underlie this is the almost complete specialization of pitch in English to demarcation and to expression of attitude. The practice of dramatic coaches in trying to control the pitch behavior of amateur actors seems to consist, almost invariably, of telling them what they are to pretend they feel about what they are saying. It is, I contend, the unfeeling use of pitch by Vietnamese speakers which cannot be casually adopted – which is what's so hard about that.

Certain types of sound-making behavior are, it would appear, much harder than others to pry loose from their original matrix for recombination in novel circumstances.

I offer this as a principle with some applicability in a wide variety of contrastive-linguistics investigations. I would hope that eventually we might devise some kind of a metric to indicate how nearly ready to fly off into another orbit a given specimen of sound-making behavior is. As a start, I think we can at least gather illustrative instances that display varying degrees of detachability.

The exculpation of contrastive linguistics[1]

CARL JAMES

Applied linguistics, like any science, advances along the dialectical path of thesis and antitheses; the syntheses are dilatory. Currently, many serious statements are challenging some cherished tenets of audiolingualism, one of which is that contrastive analysis (CA) is of great value to foreign language teaching. CA has of late been revitalized under the influence of generative-transformational grammar and the psycholinguistic theories associated with it. It is ironical that these very revitalizing forces have engendered criticism of CA, criticism not of those embellishments that CA had added to its superstructure from the new grammar, but more radical criticism, which threatens the foundations of CA.

Besides the new criticism there is the old, which has sporadically appeared in the journals – only, seemingly, to fall on deaf ears. The old criticism may be hackneyed, but it is potentially valid until it is refuted: adherents to CA should not overlook it. This seems to have been the case on the occasion of the recent Georgetown Round Table Meeting (cf. *Georgetown Monograph No. 21*, 1968) which was wholly devoted to discussions of CA. Once again, the critics were unanswered, though they reiterated the old charges, which those scholars known to be proponents of CA chose to disregard, giving their attention to none but the most peripheral (to CA) issues.

This paper is an attempt to open the CA debate, so that solutions to some problems may be sought. Although I shall attempt to refute the arguments of those who have raised criticism of CA, no disparagement of the scholarship of those individuals is intended: indeed, they earn respect for their stimulating strictures, and may themselves feel relief that they have at last been heard.

[1] This paper was prepared during 1969–70 while I was supported by a Graduate School Research Award to the Department of Language Laboratories, Faculty of Letters, University of Wisconsin, Milwaukee. I wish to acknowledge the generosity of all concerned, particularly Professor Robert F. Roeming, who always found time to discuss problems of applied linguistics with me, and from whose erudition I learned much. The errors of this paper are solely my own.

[53]

The arguments against CA will be taken in a succession which is not altogether random, though it has the disadvantages of itemization. Cross references will be made wherever it is deemed appropriate.

Arguments and counterargument

(1) *Interference from the L_1 is not the sole source of error in L_2 learning. There are other sources, which CA fails to predict. Even the unsophisticated teacher who knows no linguistics is conscious of more errors than CA can predict*

This rather weak criticism has been voiced recently by a number of scholars. S. Pit Corder (1967, p. 162) says: 'Teachers have not always been very impressed by this contribution from the linguist for the reason that their practical experience has usually already shown them where these difficulties lie and they have not felt that the contribution of the linguist has provided them with any significantly new information. They noted, for example, that many of the errors with which they were familiar were not predicted by the linguist anyway.' Wilkins (1968) restates Upshur (1962) by posing a rhetorical question: 'Yet is it true that by listing the areas of differences between languages we are listing all the linguistic difficulties that will occur? This is surely an oversimplified view.' He then goes on to say that over-generalization within the L_2 will also cause the learner to make errors, a fact which Pit Corder finds interesting as an extra indicator of transitional competence in the L_2. As if to strengthen his argument, Wilkins adds that many errors even are 'not linguistic in origin' but rather psychological and pedagogical. Lee (1968) echoes Wilkins by observing that interference will emanate not only from the L_1, but also from newly absorbed L_2 material: '...the learner...will tend to notice and produce, by false analogy, wrong patterns of that language as well as patterns of his own' (language). Dušková's valuable paper (1969) lists separately interference errors and false-analogies, and reaches the sober conclusion: 'To sum up what has been found about the source of large groups of errors, we may say that while interference from the mother tongue plays a role, it is not the only interfering factor.'

The most obvious way to answer this criticism is to point out that CA has never claimed that L_1 interference is the sole source of error. As Lado put it: 'These differences are the chief source of difficulty in learning a second language', and, 'The most important factor determining ease and difficulty in learning the patterns of a foreign language is their similarity to or difference from the patterns of the native language' (Lado 1964, pp. 21

and 91). 'Chief source' and 'most important' imply that L_1 interference is not conceived to be the only source.

Implicit in the criticisms quoted is the suggestion that there is a separate alternative to CA, namely error analysis. This is a strange type of alternative, since the two are so different in their approaches: *a priori* versus *a posteriori* detection of error. It is like the alternative: give up smoking or have the tumor removed by surgery. Pit Corder and Dušková do not hold the view that CA and error analysis are simply alternatives for achieving the same end: They rightly realize that error analysis can only become fully *explanatory* if errors coming from L_1 interference are taken into account. CA is a necessary component complementing error analysis, if errors other than false-analogies are to be taken into account. Stockwell's view (1968) is slightly different in that he does not see CA and error analysis as merely complementary. For him, there are two kinds of CA, a predictive variety typified by classical CA, and a diagnostic variety which is used in the analysis of students' errors. The relevant passage is: 'This task – comparison in search of sources of interference, commonly called contrastive analysis – can obviously be approached in either of two ways: by collecting lists of errors students have made, and then trying to describe the conflicts between the systems that give rise to such errors (not all the errors can be traced to this source, of course), or by setting up a systematic comparison which scans the differences in structure in search of sources of interference, and predicting that such-and-such errors will occur from such-and-such conflicts' (pp. 18–19). Dušková's work employs the first type: she tabulates the errors of Czechs learning English, then attempts to see which are explicable in terms of interference from the L_1.

The point of all this citation is to force a reasonable definition of error analysis. Anyone may eventually ascertain through observation which errors are recurrent in students' L_2, but that is not enough; as Hamp (1968) points out, mere enumeration of errors is taxonomic, and simply not an *analysis*; 'analysis', to be meaningful, demands an explanation of the nature and ultimate cause of observed errors. Admittedly, many of them will be explicable (or analyzable) in terms of over-generalization within the L_2, just as many will be traceable to improper training methods. But as long as some errors are plausibly explained in terms of influence of the L_1 (Dušková establishes that many are), then CA will continue to be valid, whether it be exercised in its prognostic or its diagnostic form. A further point, made by Hamp, is that we wish to be able to make statements about *potential* as well as *actual* errors: 'We want instead to develop a theory adequate to explain cases not in our corpus...We want, if you like, some kind of competence model here.' The present writer would argue that CA is a necessary component of a L_2-learning model which reliably forecasts that the speaker of an arbitrary L_1 is liable to produce grammatically deviant L_2 sentences, the structural descriptions of which will resemble those of analogous L_1 sentences.

As to the criticism that CA fails to predict those errors whose causes are non-linguistic in nature, it is not to be taken seriously. CA, as a branch of applied linguistics, has been concerned only with *linguistic* sources of error, so the criticism is no more cogent than criticizing a lawn mower on the grounds that it is useless as a combine harvester.

A simple, though non-trivial point in reply to those proposing error taxonomies as a better alternative than CA has recently been made in a published account of the cruder contrasts of Spanish and American Negro dialect with Standard American. The authors 'again found that there is a particular dearth of materials dealing with the actual English speech of Mexican-Americans or Puerto Ricans' (Politzer and Bartley 1969, p. 2). Those observant teachers who know so much about errors have been dilatory in publishing the facts: CA has been more energetic.

Finally, it will probably turn out that many of the errors which are now not traceable to the L_1, and are therefore attributed to L_2 over-generalization, will, as linguistic knowledge of deep structure develops, be recognized as errors of interference. This will be found to be particularly true for those errors which *must* now be attributed to L_2 over-generalization, being 'categories non-existent in the mother tongue' (Dušková, p. 18, No. 3.22). Thus, while Dušková finds it possible to say that there are no articles in Czech, James (1969) has suggested that such categories do exist in the Slavic languages, but at a deeper level than their Germanic counterparts.

(2) *The predictions of student errors in L_2 made by CA are not reliable*

Baird (1967) points out that in some Indian languages there is a dental [t̪] and a retroflex [t], either of which, in terms of CA, could be substituted for the English /t/ phoneme. What happens, though, is that the retroflex usually substitutes for /t/, while the dental, with aspiration added, stands in for English /θ/. Baird adds: 'It is unlikely that a contrastive study of the phonology of Hindi or Urdu and English would have enabled the teacher [sic!] to predict this choice with any certainty.' Lee (1968) misses the point of CA by citing this in criticism of CA: the choice is made for non-linguistic reasons (as Lee says) and CA is *linguistically* based (q.v.) so cannot be expected to have taken into account socio-cultural conventions. Furthermore, it is very likely that the choice of [t] for /t/ and [t̪ʰ] for /θ/ *is* linguistically determined, but linguistic analysis has not yet discovered the rules governing the choice: applied linguistics is bound by the limitations of linguistic knowledge. So Baird's and Lee's contention does not constitute a valid criticism of CA.

A similar criticism is cited by Wilkins; it concerns 'unpredictable alternation between two potential substitutions', a case in point being (Lado 1957) French speakers' propensity to substitute either French /s/, /z/ or /t/, /d/ for English /θ/, /ð/. As it stands, the CA prediction is valid: but the strict veracity of CA is being criticized. As in the preceding Indian example, it is likely that it is the paucity of linguistic knowledge that prevents CA from predicting which and when. Either that, or this is a case of interlingual free variation. As long as linguists choose to make ample use of this concept, it is not surprising that CA should be satisfied with it.

The most regrettable feature of such criticism is that it imputes to CA claims that have never been made for it: CA has never claimed to be able to predict all errors, nor has it claimed linguistic omniscience about which 'choices' speakers will make. Lado (1968, p. 125) claims no more than ability to predict 'behaviour that is likely to occur with greater than random frequency'.

(3) *CA is based on, and perpetuates, a naive view of language structure*

Lee (p. 192) informs the reader that 'A language is not a collection of separable and self-sufficient parts. The parts are mutually dependent and mutually determinative.' Newmark and Reibel (1968, p. 161) go a little farther, suggesting that CA is committed to a piecemeal theory of learning: 'to learn a new language...one bit at a time'. Recent work in generative grammar has shown that what seem to be bits of isolated language fall together at deeper levels of structure. CA is as cognisant of these findings as are the writers just quoted; we need only skim the work of Stockwell *et al.*, Nickel and Wagner, James, and the PAKS Reports (see bibliography) to see that this is so. There is another answer to the criticism: that it is the conventions for stating points of interlingual difference which give the erroneous impression that CA endorses an atomistic view of language. It is impossible to describe in a way accessible to the layman, how any two systems conform or contrast, without first itemizing the systems. Furthermore, since CAs are destined for eventual pedagogic use, whether in textbook or taped form, certain principles of sequencing and grading must be observed: obviously, an undifferentiated and monolithic entity like a language must be broken down into discrete entities for pedagogic use. It is ironic that Lee himself uses the term 'parts' in remarks about the unity of language. This is a logical constraint on exposition, not valid criticism of CA.

(4) *There are no established criteria for comparability*

Hamp (1968, p. 143) implies that CA has inadequately solved the problem of comparability: 'i.e. of establishing what is to be juxtaposed'. He further implies that the only serious attempt is that of Halliday, McIntosh and Strevens (1964), who proposed the criterion of translational equivalence. While it is true that translation is still widely used, it is not true that that has been the only serious attempt to define the criterion. Nor was Hamp's proposal for a new criterion, namely 'form and placement of rules in a grammar', new, even in 1968. Working in the T–G framework that Hamp's proposal assumes, Klima (1962) and Stockwell *et al.* (1965, though drafted by 1962) employed just that criterion. Subsequent CA work in the T–G framework has attempted to elaborate this approach, while there have been significant attempts to integrate the translation criterion explicitly with the T–G approach, proposing such factors as 'congruence' and 'equivalence' (cf. Krzeszkowski 1967 and Marton 1968). The criticism of criteria proposed can not be a valid criticism of CA in itself.

(5) *CA endorses a teacher-centred rather than a learner-centred approach to foreign language learning*

An example of such criticism is: 'The excessive preoccupation with the contribution of the teacher has then distracted the theorists from considering the role of the learner as anything but a generator of interference' (Newmark and Reibel, 1968, p. 149). This instance of criticism is a reflex of its authors' insistence (cf. *ibid.*) that the student's natural language-learning capacity will ensure success, provided he has sufficient exposure to the target language, '...if particular, whole instances of the language are modeled for him and if his own particular acts using the language are selectively reinforced'. It is difficult to see why Newmark and Reibel should have gained the impression that CA precludes the teacher's modeling of whole instances of the language; they seem to think that teachers will model only the bits that contrast with bits of the L_1, leaving the rest to chance. Teachers do model whole instances, in order to provide context for the bits that they assume will be troublesome. The fact that the context (or, better, Halliday's 'co-texts') varies does not mean that it is considered unimportant: Any linguist knows that an item's co-text is part and parcel of the definition of that item. The reason why teachers proceed in this way is that they believe that the learner's 'particular acts' stand a better chance of being reinforceable if they are elicited under conditions conducive to success. CA holds the view that such conditions should be built into the teaching strategy. None of this detracts from the dignity of the learner, and adherents of CA would agree that in the last analysis it is the student who learns: the teacher cannot learn for him, but he can provide optimal conditions for learning, as Horace Mann observed in his report of 1838: 'Though much must be done by others to aid, yet the effective labour must be performed by the learner himself...It is the duty of the teacher to bring knowledge within arm's length of the learner; and he breaks down its masses into portions so minute that they can be taken up and appropriated one by one; but the final appropriating act must be the learner's.' To abandon teaching in favour of random exposure to that which needs to be taught is to reject the foundations of educational philosophy.

Hadlich (1965) suggests that CA is so teacher-centred that it concocts problems for the learner. This is a very serious accusation. He is concerned with lexis, and claims that problem pairs like Spanish *salir/dejar* are non-native: with this we concur. 'The relation between the members of each pair is extraneous to the language being studied...imposed on the foreign language from without.' We are told that Spaniards don't find the pair *salir/dejar* difficult; nor does the Englishman stumble over *do/make*: they are not even pairs for the native. Of course they are not. But the learner of Spanish is 'extraneous' to Spanish, or he would not need to learn it, and CA is interested in language contact, not in languages in isolation. If CA could assume that a L_2 could be learned in isolation, as the L_1 is learned, then Hadlich's strictures would be valid: such an assumption seems untenable, however. Hadlich ascribes the problem-making effect of CA to translation. We have shown above that translation is a criterion for comparability in CA, but it is certainly not a teaching technique, as Hadlich thinks. All traces of translation are erased from a CA, long before the textbook based on that CA reaches the classroom. It has been explicitly stated for CA that translation is a hindrance to fluency (James 1969, p. 91). It must be stated quite categorically that CA is *not* a method, and such a phrase as Hadlich's 'taught contrastively' (p. 429, col. 1) is a misnomer. Either that, or Hadlich is using 'contrastive' in a different sense from that normal in CA. That such is the case is clear from his examples; he uses *Salí de casa* and *Dejé el sombrero* to illustrate the contrast (i.e. CA-type contrast) between the two verbs, but he then goes on to warn of the danger of 'erroneous substitution' (p. 427), as if there were two-minimal pair-phrases in Spanish in which *salir* and *dejar* were contrastively (in his sense) interchangeable. Since there is no such minimal pair in Spanish, the problem pair is not a lexical one, in which case CA would take the distributional constraints into account; so CA and Hadlich would be doing the same thing.

One point implicit in Hadlich's minatory remark that 'awareness of the possibility of erroneous substitution fosters in itself the substitution it is designed to forestall' is partly true and interesting. It concerns the possibility of *overcompensation*, a good example being that of Haugen (1956), who reports that Spanish speakers learning English *some, sun, sung*, will at first identify all the sounds as /n/, because of the L_1. CA would predict this as a 'perception blind spot'. With teaching they will learn to distinguish the sounds, but through anxiety they overcompensate, producing /sʌŋ/ for *sun*, although final /n/ exists in Spanish and so should present no difficulty. Notice that it is not the 'very substitution' that is made (Hadlich) but the inverse substitution. It is interesting that this involves backward interference, from the L_2 to the speaker's transitional competence (cf. Pit Corder) of the L_2. Language learning then seems, at times, to be a *tri*lingual process, the three 'languages' being: L_1 – Transitional L_2 – L_2 model. The same phenomenon occurs in dialect situations, and its effects are termed 'hyperurbanisms'. The Yorkshireman, embarrassed by his dialectal inelegant /ʊ/ in *butter*, substitutes the more respectable [ə] for RP /ʌ/, whereupon he overcompensates on the /ʊ/ → /ə/ ~ /ʌ/ rule to produce /kəd/, /kəʃn/ for *could, cushion*. The parallelism with the Spanish example can be shown thus:

L_1 Spanish inventory	Transitional competence	Target inventory (English)
/-n/ only	//-ŋ/ only	/-n/ and /-ŋ/
/ʊ/ only	/ʌ/ (/ə/) only	/ʊ/ and /ʌ/
Yorkshire inventory	Transitional competence	Target inventory (RP)

This suggests that L_1:L_2 conflict produces an intermediary language form, for which 'transitional competence' is a good label. The proposal that this *third* language could be provisionally set up as a bridge between L_1 and L_2 has been made in James (1969, p. 91) in an article on CA. One additional point to the Yorkshire example is that such 'erroneous substitution' occurs in a natural unscripted language-learning setting, so it cannot be blamed on CA in that case.

(6) The example quoted provides a part answer to a common criticism of interference theory: *CA only conceives of interference in one direction, from L_1 to L_2.*

CA has emphasized this direction of interference, and rightly so, since it is the form most prevalent in L_2 learning, and after all, CA is interested in teaching the L_2, not the L_1. References to backward interference are not hard to find in the literature. Jakobovits (1969) has described the general principles of transfer, including the case where the relationship between the two languages (R $L_1 - L_2$) has a particular value, as with related languages: the L_1 will be influenced by the L_2. Such influence he vividly terms *Backlash* interference and adds (p. 70) that it 'is expected to be strongest at later stages of L_2 learning and to be minimal at the beginning'. Usually, the cognitive effects of L_2 learning are stressed (e.g. Macnamara), but Jakobovits is explicit on the linguistic effects: 'Upon learning a second language, the individual may come to adopt new cognitive, attitudinal, *as well as linguistic modes of functioning* (my italics). Teachers frequently notice that the L_2 interferes with their students' L_2, when they write 'schul' and 'telefon' under the influence of German and Spanish. When translating orally from German, they let stand such words as 'deutsch' or 'damit'; that is, they adopt them into the L_1, or into the transitional L_2. In writing English, the present author frequently writes 'wend', 'tob' for 'went' and 'top' as if under the spell of *Auslautsverhärtung*. As Dodson points out in his remarkable and seemingly underread book (1967, p. 90): 'It is only possible to teach a second language by direct-method techniques [such as Newmark and Reibel are in essence promoting – C. J.] at the expense of the first language and it is sheer hypocrisy to claim that the final aim of such teaching philosophies is bilingualism.' Add to this the common experience of trying to learn a *third* language: unless the L_2 is almost as well known as the L_1, it is unable to resist interference (backward) from the L_3, and is quite rapidly ousted by it. Nor do the L_2 and L_3 need to be resemblant: the writer has experienced the effect when learning Spanish on top of Polish. Notice that such effects occur *whilst learning*, so they do not fall under the category mislabeled interference, which should more properly be termed forgetting (a category conceded by Newmark and Reibel).

(7) Having turned our attention to L_3 learning situations, we can deal with another argument advanced to discredit interference theory. It runs something like this: *We expect the strongest habits to exert most interference, so why is it that the weaker L_2 habits interfere more with the L_3 than L_1 habits?*

The answer is possibly that the L_2 exerts *high level* influence on the L_3, affecting such high level features as phonotactics, allophonics, and lexis. The interference from L_1 remains, and affects low level features, to which, however, less attention has been paid than to the high level ones. They are in a sense less startling than the latter, superficial deviations. Another answer involves the notion of psychological 'set': the learner realizes that success in foreign language performance involves excluding the L_1, as far as he is consciously able to, and feels that anything is better for foreign language performance than L_1 material. He is successful in excluding the L_1 on the psychomotor level, but not on the cognitive level. This is probably the explanation of Lee's difficulty with Spanish and Italian, though his anecdote was meant to prove a different point, which we now turn to.

(8) *The degree of typological difference between L_1 and L_2 is not proportional to the interference strength*

The traditional CA standpoint is stated by Barrutia (1967, p. 24): 'It was not an unexpected discovery to find that these interferences are considerably less between languages of the same immediate origin and increase in relative proportion as the more distant languages mesh in a common but far-removed source language such as proto Indo-European.' In other words, it will be more difficult for a Spanish speaker to learn Chinese than Italian, since these two languages are at the opposite extremes of isomorphism with his L_1, so he needs to transfer less and learn more when he learns Chinese, and can transfer more and learn less when Italian is his target. That some languages are harder to learn than others, given a certain L_1 as a starting point, is generally accepted. Cleveland *et al.* (1960), speaking for English L_1 students, point out that *French, German, Rumanian, Spanish* and *Italian* are learned in two-thirds of the time needed to achieve the same proficiency in *Russian, Greek, Finnish*, and in half the time needed for *Chinese, Japanese* and *Vietnamese*. Since it seems that some languages are not intrinsically more difficult than others, especially if the Japanese speaker learns Vietnamese more quickly than German, we must conclude that the L_1 is the crux of the matter. The explanation can hardly be that the 'hard' languages are hard because they are taught less well than the easy ones, for we do not attest relativity of success among the languages that are traditionally taught in Europe, say. British teachers are not aware, that is, that Spanish is taught better than German, or the German teachers would have learned by now the secrets of the success of their Spanish-teaching colleagues. Those who attack CA, wishing to use random exposure methods, would share the view that the reason for relative ease of learning one language over another is not to be found in the teaching, since they want to abandon teaching altogether, it seems.

The evidence available does confirm assumption of CA that it is the L_1

which determines whether any particular L_2 will be hard or easy. But Lee is adamant, insisting that learning Chinese lifted him into a new orbit of non-interference, and although he admits that 'it would probably be absurd to suggest that this ever happens', he nevertheless suggests it. One wonders where Lee stands in the field of language-learning theory: between the two stools of innate ideas and a L_2 *tabula rasa*, evidently. We would reply in this way: When the Italian learns Spanish, he has a lot in his L_1 to fall back on, but in learning Chinese he has nothing. If he wishes to learn the L_2 he must at all costs perform in that language, and as soon as he starts to perform he will fall back on the L_1: there is no free will for him. His falling back jeopardizes his L_2 performance more when it is Chinese than when it is Spanish: this is interference.[1] A possible counter-argument to my suggestion is: learn the L_2 through the L_2 only. This implies keeping out the L_1 for some reason or other: the only reason I can discover is – to avert interference. So we come back full circle to interference, which was the reason for starting the argument. Implicit in the 'stay within L_2' argument is a naive view of language, moreover. It might be just possible to avert interference by learning all L_2 material parrot-wise, or, as H. E. Palmer (1917, p. 103) put it, as *Primary* matter. Now, since the number of possible sentences in a language is infinite, reliance on primary matter, learned atomistically, is not a feasible way to learn a language, since the human life-span is too short. So the learner must learn to produce his own *Secondary* matter from the small amount of primary matter that he can memorize, 'by some process of substitution, transformation, or other combination' (Politzer 1965). This applies *a fortiori* where an L_2 *tabula rasa* is posited. In the newer T–G theory of CA, it is the routes by which one proceeds from primary to secondary matter which determine the degree of L_1 interference. The Italian will have more success in following L_1 routes to produce L_2 secondary matter if the L_2 is Spanish than if it is Chinese: interference will be greater in the second case. CA-based teaching materials are designed to ensure that L_1 routes to L_2 secondary matter are followed only where the results will be good.

The foregoing argument is of particular topical pertinence to the work being undertaken in the U.S.A. and in Britain (by Le Page at York) on dialect expansion: speakers of a non-standard dialect of English (D_1) are being taught a standard dialect (D_2) as a means to economic and social

---

[1] Lado's view on this is clear. On the subject of learning a new alphabet, he writes: 'Between English and Korean there will be no major negative transfer such as would result if some symbols were similar but represented different sounds. *And there will be no positive transfer* as when similar symbols represent similar sounds' (Lado, 1957 p. 106, italics supplied).

betterment. For two language forms to qualify as dialects of the same language, they must share many features. If Lee's contention (q.v.) were valid, it would be harder to learn another dialect of one's own language than to learn a foreign language; but this is not the case, as people learn new dialects all the time. Those involved in planning dialect-expansion in the U.S.A. are preparing CAs of D_1 and D_2. These CAs seem to be motivated academically and linguistically rather than pedagogically, but this author has heard the claim made[1] that CA is probably more relevant to dialect teaching than to language teaching. This seems to be overstating the case, and is a reflection of the zeal with which dialect linguists are working to establish for the D_1 parity of linguistic status with the Standard. Yet in one sense at least a dialect CA *can* contribute more than a L_1–L_2 CA, but pre-pedagogically. That is, the first type of CA can do much by discovering the (minor) ways in which the dialects differ, so that the rest, which is also the most, can be left out of the teaching. Thus, it will determine the *matter* to be taught, not strategies for teaching, as is the case in language CA. In all events, dialect comparison, when compared itself to language comparison, adds another linguistic theoretical dimension to CA as we presently know it.

(9) *Interference is an otiose idea: ignorance is the real cause of error*

By far the most valuable criticism of interference theory – and therefore of CA – to date is that of Newmark and Reibel (1968): valuable because, unlike the other strictures here examined, it offers an alternative explanation of errors made in L_2 learning. Newmark and Reibel insist that errors are caused by inadequate knowledge of the target language: when the learner is 'induced to perform' in the L_2 'there are many things he has not yet learned to do...What can he do other than use what he already knows to make up for what he does not know?' While this explanation is made with reference to 'the phenomenon of foreign accent', which is manifest at the psycho-motor level of performance (cf. Carroll 1968), it is presumably intended to embrace all interference, even at the cognitive level. It is also presumably meant to apply to both productive and receptive interference; but it is rather more acceptable for the former than the latter. That is, it seems plausible to suggest that if I fail to hear a certain L_2 sound, i.e. if I have a 'perception blind spot' (Lado 1957), then I will assume I have heard the nearest L_1 equivalent: so I have indeed filled a L_2 lacuna with L_1 material. But to extend the analogy, to productive filling-in, is not easy,

---

[1] Robert O. H. Petersen, Director of the Hilo Language Development Project (Hawaii), would claim this (personal communication).

since it would require the learner-speaker to 'define' his own L_2 goals, and then fall short of these goals in his performance. The objection is: if he can define the goal, he is, properly speaking, not ignorant of the L_2.

The ignorance theory is vulnerable on another count: what is meant by 'knowledge' of a target language? Surely analytic knowledge of L_2 rules etc. is not what is meant, but rather skills or manipulative knowledge. Newmark and Reibel are ambivalent on this issue: they speak of '...things ...he has not learned to do' (= skill?) and in the next breath of 'what he does not know' (= analytic?). Now it is widely accepted that having analytic knowledge of a L_2 will not produce the required behaviour equatable with such knowledge: 'English speaking students know that the Spanish word is [teléfono] from their first encounter with it, but English stress interference will still produce many a [teléfono] and require numerous corrections before the proper habit sets in' (Barrutia). We presume that Newmark and Reibel intend by 'knowledge' the unformulated consciousness of linguistic rules which determine acceptable performance, namely *competence*. So they are saying that learners' performance is bad because their competence is bad: nobody would disagree.

Ignorance theory is only ostensibly an alternative to interference theory. If we provisionally accept interference, for the sake of argument, we will concede that at a given stage of L_2 learning, certain L_2 items need to be learnt, i.e. the learner is ignorant of those L_2 items. Suppose we now do not explicitly introduce one of those L_2 items, yet insist that the learner perform a repertoire including that L_2 item: 'faute de mieux' he will use the closest L_1 item. So far, the competing theories agree: they differ only as to whether using the L_1 item is attributable to ignorance of the L_2 or to the influence of the L_1 – the argument is otiose, like which came first: chicken or egg?

No language-learning or language-teaching theory has ever envisaged the state of affairs where the learner is asked to perform before he has had some chance to gain 'knowledge' of the L_2 target item. All theories, even those promulgated by the theorists whom Newmark and Reibel disparage, presuppose that the L_2 item shall be introduced – the vague term 'introduce' is selected intentionally, to allow for conflicting theories of introduction, whether it be effected by exposure to or by explanation of L_2 items. The fact is that teachers have discovered that with equal amounts of 'introduction', the learner gains 'knowledge' of some items more easily and quickly than others. This variable can only be attributed – if such others as teaching skill, motivation, etc. are kept constant – to the L_1, whether or not the L_2 item is in some amenable form present in the L_1. If extrapolation from the L_1 is disastrous, one can say that the learner is 'ignorant' (L_1-wise) of the L_2 form required. One can equally well say that his failure to produce an acceptable L_2 form is the result of his L_1 having led him up a blind alley: this is usually termed *interference*. Thus, ignorance and interference become synonymous. Where extrapolation from the L_1 is successful, there is no interference, and *apparently* no ignorance either: yet L_2-wise, the learner is equally ignorant of the L_2 form, whether his performance be successful or calamitous.

We can emphasize the point just made by reference to the distinction already made (8) between easy and hard languages. If the ignorance theory were legitimate, we would have to concede that the Italian learner's ignorance of Chinese and of Spanish were at the outset equal. This being the case, why should he find acceptable performance in the one more easily attainable than in the other? One would have to say that he combats his ignorance more easily in one case than the other. Since Chinese is inherently no harder than Spanish, it can hardly be the case that L_2-internal analogizing is consistently more reliable in Spanish than in Chinese: this would be tantamount to saying that some languages are more systematic and logical than others – which is anathema in modern linguistics! We have no choice but to bring in the L_1, and with the L_1 comes interference.

This paper has been an attempt to examine critically some recurrent strictures on the logical foundation of, and hence the continued practice of, CA in language teaching. It is possible that the counterarguments voiced here have often been made, and in turn themselves been refuted in the ivory towers of our discipline: but the present writer is unaware of any document which sets the arguments out in a form rendering them available to the wider public of applied linguistics. This paper is not meant to be provocative, though it is to be hoped that it will stimulate discussion of the topic in hand.

References

Baird, A. (1967). 'Contrastive studies and the language teacher', *English Language Teaching* XXI.

Barrutia, R. (1967). 'Dispelling the myth', *Modern Language Journal* LI, 1.

Carroll, J. B. (1968). 'Contrastive linguistics and interference theory', *Georgetown Monograph No. 21*.

Cleveland, H., Mangone, G. J. and Adams, J. C. (1960). *The Overseas Americans*, McGraw Hill, New York.

Corder, S. Pit (1967). 'The significance of learners' errors', *IRAL* v, 4.

Dodson, C. J. (1967). *Language Teaching and the Bilingual Method*, Pitman, London.

Dušková, L. (1969). 'On sources of errors in foreign language learning', *IRAL* VII, 1.

Hadlich, R. L. (1965). 'Lexical contrastive analysis', *Modern Language Journal* XLIX, 7.

Halliday, M. A. K., McIntosh, A. and Strevens, P. D. (1964). *The Linguistic Sciences and Language Teaching*.

Hamp, E. P. (1968). 'What a contrastive grammar is not, if it is', *Georgetown Monograph No. 21*.

Haugen, E. (1956). *Bilingualism in the Americas*, American Dialect Society.

Jakobovits, L. A. (1969). 'Second language learning and transfer theory: a theoretical assessment', *Language Learning* XIX, 1, 2.

James, Carl (1969). 'Deeper contrastive study', *IRAL* VII, 2.

Klima, E. S. (1962). 'Correspondence at the grammatical level', MIT Research Laboratory of Electronics XXIV, *Mechanical Translation*.

Krzeszkowski, T. (1967). 'Fundamental principles of structural contrastive studies', *Glottodidactica* II.

Lado, R. (1957). *Linguistics across Cultures*, Ann Arbor, Michigan.

   (1964). *Language Teaching: A Scientific Approach*, McGraw Hill, New York.

   (1968). 'Contrastive linguistics in a mentalistic theory of language learning', in *Georgetown Monograph No. 21*.

Lee, W. R. (1968). 'Thoughts on contrastive linguistics in the context of language teaching', *Georgetown Monograph No. 21*.

Mann, Horace (1965). Report on Massachusetts Schools, quoted in H. Diack, *In Spite of the Alphabet*, Chatto and Windus, pp. 50–2.

Marton, W. (1968). 'Equivalence and congruence in transformational contrastive studies', *Studia-Anglica Poznaniensia* I.

Newmark, L. and Reibel, D. A. (1968). 'Necessity and sufficiency in language learning', *IRAL* VI, 3.

Nickel, G. and Wagner, K. H. (1968). 'Contrastive linguistics and language learning', *IRAL* VI, 3.

PAKS Reports: Projekt für Angewandte Kontrastive Sprachwissenschaft, G. Nickel, Director.

Palmer, H. E. (1917). *The Scientific Study and Teaching of Languages*. London, Harrap.

Politzer, R. L. (1965). 'Some reflections on transfer of training in foreign language learning', *IRAL* III, 3.

Politzer, R. L. and Bartley, D. E. (1969). *Standard English and Nonstandard Dialects: Elements of Syntax*, Research Memorandum No. 54, Stanford University, School of Education.

Stockwell, R. P. (1968). 'Contrastive analysis and lapsed time', in *Georgetown Monograph No. 21*.

Stockwell, R. P., Bowen, J. D. and Martin, J. W. (1965). *The Grammatical Structures of English and Spanish*, Chicago.

Upshur, J. A. (1962). 'Language proficiency testing and the contrastive analysis dilemma', *Language Learning* XII, 2.

Wilkins, D. A. (1968). Review of A. Valdman (ed.), *Trends in Language Teaching*, *IRAL* VI, 1.

Grammatical variability and the difference between native and non-native speakers

ILSE LEHISTE

A currently popular method of teaching syntactic theory involves contrastive presentation of 'grammatical' and 'non-grammatical' sentences. There is, however, increasing evidence that native speakers do not agree among themselves about what is grammatical (Elliott, Legum and Thompson 1969; Quirk and Svartvik 1966). The use of the criterion of grammaticality may therefore be questioned on theoretical grounds. A concrete problem arises in teaching a syntax course to a group of students including both native and non-native speakers of the language from which the examples are drawn: non-native speakers frequently fail to see the rationale for a particular decision as to whether a sentence is or is not grammatical, if this rationale consists of an appeal to the native speaker's intuition.

The notion of grammaticality is admittedly difficult to define, and even more difficult to explain to linguistically naive users of a language (Bolinger 1968). One way to explore the reliability of native speakers' grammaticality judgments would be to compare the actual use of a grammatical feature by a group of monolingual native speakers of English with the use of the same feature by a group of bilinguals for whom English is the second language. In this manner, direct reference to grammaticality would be avoided.

I conducted a small experiment, the purpose of which was to compare the ranges of grammatical variability within two such groups, with the view of finding out whether the difference between the two groups, if any, was significantly different from the variation within the native group.

I selected a set of 91 English sentences which had already been used to test the range of variability within a group of native speakers of English (Langendoen 1970). The subjects of this study were a group of junior high and high school teachers of English, who participated in a summer institute

[69]

at Ohio State University in 1968. The structural feature which the sentences were designed to test was the formation of 'tag questions'. This term is used to refer to questions asking for confirmation of the content of a declarative sentence. For example, the statement 'The sky looks threatening' might be followed by 'doesn't it', which would constitute an appropriate tag question. The responses given by the 46 native speakers are analyzed in detail in Langendoen's forthcoming book. A gross indication of the amount of grammatical variability found within this group is provided by the fact that the test subjects showed complete agreement in only 33 instances out of 91. In the other cases, the number of different responses to a single statement varied between two and eight.

I presented the same set of sentences to a comparable group of 46 Estonian–English bilinguals ranging in age from 17 to 51. The bilinguals, who are long-term residents of the United States and Canada, took the same test under similar conditions. The particular structural feature, formation of tag questions, is very suitable for testing with this group, since Estonian does not know tag questions of the English kind; a statement might be turned into a question by the use of a phrase similar to the German *nicht wahr* or the French *n'est-ce pas*, but even that would not be very common. The older bilinguals have Estonian as first language and English as second language both in order of acquisition and in order of fluency. The younger members of the group have learned Estonian from their parents and English from the surrounding community, and consider themselves to be more fluent in English than in Estonian. Almost all bilinguals use English in more situations than Estonian, although most of them continue to speak Estonian within their immediate family. The educational level of the bilingual group is at least comparable to that of the monolingual group, and all bilinguals have had some formal instruction in English grammar; they cannot, however, be expected to be as familiar with formalized 'school grammar' as the monolingual group consisting of teachers of the English language.

I started out with the expectation that there would be considerable variation within the bilingual group, and that the younger bilinguals would be progressively more similar to the native speakers of English than the older bilinguals in their formation of tag questions. I hoped to find a way to express the degree of similarity in some concrete terms which might be used as a measure of 'degree of bilingualism' or, perhaps, 'degree of nativeness'. I should say from the outset that the results of the experiment turned out largely negative.

In order to establish some measure of the degree of similarity between the two groups, I arbitrarily defined the notion of 'deviant response' as a variant of a tag question not included among the set of variants offered by the members of the monolingual group in response to a specific sentence calling for confirmation. For example, if the statement was 'The boy looks sleepy' and all 46 native speakers formed the tag questions 'doesn't he', then a bilingual's 'does he not' was classified as a deviant response. (Later I shall present a more detailed analysis of deviant responses.)

A gross comparison of the two sets of 4,186 tag questions yielded 701 deviant responses on the part of the bilinguals, amounting to 16·7% of the total. A separate analysis of 23 younger members of the group, below the median age of 27 years, showed 297 deviant responses; the 23 older members had 404 deviant responses. Thus the younger bilinguals contributed about 42% of the deviant responses, while the older half of the group was responsible for 58% of the deviations. This difference does not seem to be particularly striking.

A separate analysis of the deviant responses of each bilingual subject showed that the number of deviant responses ranged from one to 68 (out of 91). A large proportion of deviant responses was furnished by six individuals, whose scores were 68, 62, 54, 54, 41 and 35. The curve became fairly smooth after that. It is perhaps significant that the subgroup of six contained the two oldest members of the group; but these were balanced out by an 18-year-old and a 19-year-old at the other extreme of the age range. Together, the six subjects with the highest number of deviations accounted for almost half of the difference between the monolinguals and the bilinguals. If these six individuals were discounted, there would remain less than ten deviant responses for each remaining bilingual.

It is of course questionable whether the notion 'deviant response' has any validity at all. It should be kept in mind that there was extensive variability within the monolingual group, even though it consisted of English teachers. This variability was reflected in the number of possible responses to a given statement, which ranged from one to eight. There is no evidence as to how a less uniform monolingual group would have performed under similar circumstances, and what the number of their deviant responses might be relative to the responses given by the reference group. It is likewise unknown whether the same two groups would have produced identical responses when re-tested on a different occasion. As I emphasized before, the counting of deviant responses constitutes only a very gross measure of the differences between the younger and the older half of the bilingual group on the one hand, and between the monolingual and the bilingual groups, on the other. With these reservations in mind,

I cannot consider the differences in any way conclusive, and the starting hypothesis does not appear to be confirmed.

Let us look now a little more closely at the deviant responses. In fact many of the apparent deviations have no linguistic significance. The monolingual group, being English teachers, had a clear notion of what a tag question is: the bilingual group seemed to have considerable difficulty in grasping what was required of them, and many of their responses suggest that the subjects must have thought they were participating in a free association test. For example, all monolinguals responded to the sentence 'I have five cents in my pocket' with either 'Haven't I?' or 'Don't I?', but two of the bilinguals asked 'How much do you have?'. There were altogether 95 deviant responses of this type.

Another set of discountable deviant responses consisted of elsewhere acceptable variants that did not occur among the monolinguals' responses at a given time. On numerous occasions, the variants of tag questions given by monolinguals might include 'don't they' and 'do they not' in response to one sentence, but only 'don't they' in response to an analogous sentence. The bilinguals may have used 'do they not' as a variant in both instances; it would have been accepted in one case, and treated as a deviant response in the other. This applies in particular to lack of inversion with regard to negation or affirmation. The general rule of the formation of tag questions requires that the statement and the tag question oppose each other with respect to negation, but there were many exceptions to this rule within both the monolingual and the bilingual group. Again, an exception to the rule within the bilingual group was counted as a deviant response if there were no exceptions within the monolingual group with regard to a given sentence. It seems to be that all such cases should be considered together, and if exceptions to a general rule occur within the monolingual group, analogous exceptions within the bilingual group should be excluded from the list of deviant responses.

The majority of the bilinguals' deviant responses fell into the two categories just described – 'free association' deviations and elsewhere acceptable variants. If these two categories are excluded, as I believe they should be, there is very little left to indicate a possible difference between the monolingual native speakers and the bilingual non-native speakers of English.

The residual difference consists of two types of deviant responses. There were, first of all, five responses that seem to translate the Estonian equivalent of *nicht wahr* or *n'est-ce pas*. These included two occurrences of *isn't it so?*, two instances of *right?*, and one occurrence of *no?*. The ages of the subjects who provided these responses ranged from 19 to 35; the 35-year-old individual provided both *isn't it so* responses.

And there were 27 pronoun references in which *he* was used for *she* and vice versa. This is a deviation which could be attributed to an Estonian substratum, since there is no grammatical gender in Estonian, and there is only one form for the pronoun of the third person. Sixteen of these 27 instances occurred in the bilinguals' responses to the sentence 'My uncle's spouse won't eat caviar'. Evidently 'My uncle's spouse' did not equal 'My uncle's wife' for the individuals who referred to 'my uncle's spouse' as 'he', and the deviance may be a matter of lexical limitation rather than a matter of being unsure in the selection of the proper masculine or feminine pronoun.

If the mistakes with regard to 'my uncle's spouse' are discounted, the concrete, quantizable differences between the monolingual and the bilingual group consist of five translated *nicht wahr* responses and eleven wrongly chosen pronouns, which would contribute about 0·4% of the 4,186 responses. To these might be added a greater grammatical variability: within the bilingual group, the number of possible responses varied between 2 and 13, whereas among the monolinguals, the number of variant responses ranged between 1 and 8. One should, however, at least consider the possibility that this greater variability might be due to the lesser degree of homogeneity within the bilingual group.

And then there are the six individuals who seem to have selected the statistically less frequent responses in a relatively great number of times. While each individual deviant response used by these six may be explained and accounted for, their very accumulation leaves a definite non-native impression. I cannot find any more precise way to define this lack of nativeness, much less express its degree in a quantizable way.

I would like to return now to the question of the grammaticality of the tag questions used by the monolingual and bilingual speakers. Langendoen's study of the responses used by the monolingual group revealed extensive variability within that group. My study of the responses used by the bilingual group has shown similar variability within the bilingual group, and a rather small difference between the two groups. Yet we speak confidently of the native speaker's unerring ability to determine what is grammatical in his language. If there is so much variation among the native speakers and so much similarity between native and non-native speakers, the appeal to the native speaker's intuitive knowledge of grammaticality seems to lose much of its force.

References

Bolinger, Dwight (1968). 'Judgments of grammaticality', *Lingua* 21, 34–40.
Elliott, Dale, Stanley Legum and Sandra Annear Thompson (1969). 'Syntactic variation as linguistic data', *Papers from the Fifth Regional Meeting of the Chicago Linguistic Society*, Department of Linguistics, University of Chicago, Chicago, Illinois, pp. 52–9.
Langendoen, D. Terence (1970). *Essentials of English Grammar*, Holt, Rinehart and Winston, New York.
Quirk, Randolph and Jan Svartvik (1966). *Investigating Linguistic Acceptability*, Mouton, The Hague.

Deep structure in a contrastive transformational grammar

JAMES L. WYATT

Not long after transformational grammars had been first produced, a contrastive transformational grammar was devised. Paul Schachter produced 'A Contrastive Analysis of English and Pangasinan' in 1959.[1] Shortly thereafter, other contrastive transformational grammars appeared. These grammars consisted of separate grammars for each language linked by statements, formulas, or charts showing equivalences.

Another type of contrastive transformational grammar[2] follows more closely the ideas of a transfer grammar as set forth by Zelig S. Harris[3] before the advent of the transformationists. That type of grammar consists of a core of rules common to two languages, and appended to that core are rules peculiar to each separate language. One would have a grammar of either language with the common core and the appended rules peculiar to that language. The common core is neutral, as far as direction from one language to the other is concerned. Direction exists if an attempt is made in the appended single language rules to account for all sentence structures in one language but not necessarily in the other. A non-directional grammar exists if all sentence structures in each language are accounted for.

This paper will illustrate how deep structure can be formulated in a common-core transformational grammar. The term *deep structure* as used here is meant to designate the source or sources of sentence elements and their manipulation to create the basis of a new and different sentence. Examples are adaptations from the writer's tentative, and therefore still experimental, Spanish–English and Portuguese–English transformational

---

[1] Paul Schachter, 'A contrastive analysis of English and Pangasinan', unpublished Ph.D. dissertation, the University of California at Los Angeles, 1959.

[2] See James L. Wyatt, 'The common-core transformational grammar: a contrastive model', *Journal of English as a Second Language* II, 2; 51–65, 1967.

[3] Zelig S. Harris, 'Transfer grammar', *International Journal of American Linguistics*, XX, 4; 259–70, 1954.

grammars. These grammars are directional in that they seek to generate practically all basic sentence structures in Spanish and Portuguese and express them in at least one 'equivalent' way in English. The writer has made no attempt to generate all basic English structures.

The rules here have been devised to cover only the source strings cited. More complicated source strings would require more elaborate rules on some occasions. The notation used here has been elaborated for this occasion in the hope that it will be easy to follow. The writer is well aware of the frustration born of an attempt to fathom symbols and notational intricacies when seen in a particular treatment of grammar. The numbering of the rules is according to the following plan: The digit before the first period refers to the main category of the transformation. In the first example, the first digit refers to the passive transformation. The digit following the first period refers to the steps in bringing the transformation about, and the digits to the right of the second period identify the rules appended to the common core for one or the other language, as indicated by the capital letter following the digit, E for English, P for Portuguese, and S for Spanish. Optional steps of the transformation are designated by indented headings. Symbols and abbreviations used here have the following meanings: Subj = subject, V_{tr} = transitive verb, DO = direct object, IO = indirect object, V_{pass} = passive verb, $Prep_{agent}$ = agentive preposition, past part = past participle, 3p = third person, $Prep_{io}$ = indirect object preposition, $Interrog_{inanimate}$ = inanimate interrogative word, $V_{interrog}$ = the English interrogative word *do* which operates like a verb, $V_{trimper}$ = transitive verb which serves as the source of an imperative. The notational system here varies somewhat from the usual transformational notation. Plus signs precede elements in a string, an influence from tagmemic notation. Underlining in source and resulting strings delimits elements for which symbols stand, and parentheses enclose optional elements. Curved braces precede obligatory choices between or among alternates.

First, we shall see how the passive transformation might be formulated as part of a Spanish–English common core transformational grammar.

1. Passive (Spanish–English)

Let *x* and its primes equal any other elements or null. (*x'* includes, among other elements, tense and person markers to be attached to the end of the first verb form.)

1.1 $x + \text{Subj} + x' + V_{tr} + \text{DO} + (\text{IO}) + x'' \rightarrow$
         Source strings

A friend took	a letter	(to John)
Subj $x' + V_{tr}$	DO	IO
Un amigo *(le) llevó	una carta	(a Juan)
Subj $x' + V_{tr}$	DO	IO

* The rule here does not account for the redundant indirect object pronoun matching the noun phrase indirect object.

$$x + \text{Subj}' : \text{DO} + x' + V_{pass} + \text{-Marker}_{past\ part} + V_{tr} +$$
$$(\text{IO}) + (\text{Prep}_{agent} + \text{Agent: Subj}) + x''$$

1.2 $V_{pass} \to \begin{cases} (E)\ V_{pass} \\ (S)\ V_{pass} \end{cases}$

1.2.1E   (E) $V_{pass} \to \underline{be}$

1.2.1S   (S) $V_{pass} \to \underline{se}$

1.3 $\text{-Marker}_{past\ part} \to \begin{cases} (E)\text{-Marker}_{past\ part} \\ (S)\text{-Marker}_{past\ part} \end{cases}$

1.3.1E   (E)-Marker$_{past\ part} \to \underline{\text{-en}}$

1.3.1S   (S)-Marker$_{past\ part} \to \begin{cases} \begin{cases} \underline{\text{-do}} \\ \underline{\text{-da}} \end{cases} \\ \begin{cases} \text{-dos} \\ \text{-das} \end{cases} \end{cases}$

The rewrite choices here depend on the gender and number of the subject.

1.4 $\text{Prep}_{agent} \to \begin{cases} (E)\ \text{Prep}_{agent} \\ (S)\ \text{Prep}_{agent} \end{cases}$

1.4.1E   (E) Prep$_{agent} \to \underline{by}$

1.4.1S   (S) Prep$_{agent} \to \underline{por}$

Resulting strings

A letter was	taken	(to John)
Subj′: DO $x' + V_{pass}$ -Marker$_{past\ part} + V_{tr}$	IO	
	(by	a friend)
	Prep$_{agent}$	Agent: Subj

Una carta	(le) fue	llevada	(a Juan)
Subj′: DO	$x' + V_{pass}$	-Marker$_{past\ part} + V_{tr}$	IO
	(por	un amigo)	
	Prep$_{agent}$	Agent: Subj	

Optional

1.4.2S $x + \text{Subj}^{3p} + x' + V_{\text{pass}} + \text{-Marker}_{\text{past part}} + V_{\text{tr}} + (\text{IO}) +$
$(\text{Prep}_{\text{agent}} + \text{Agent}) + x'' \rightarrow$

Source string

Una carta fue	llevada	(a Juan)
Subj $x' + V_{\text{pass}}$	$\text{-Marker}_{\text{past part}} + V_{\text{tr}}$	IO

(por   un amigo)
Prep$_{\text{agent}}$ Agent

$x + \underline{se} + x' + V_{\text{tr}} + \text{Subj}^{3p}$ (IO)
Resulting string

Se llevó	una carta	(a Juan)
$x' + V_{\text{tr}}$	Subj	IO

Another rule could follow here to allow for a singular verb with a plural subject, as in *Se ve las luces* 'The lights are seen'.

Optional

1.4.2E $x + \text{Subj} + x' + V_{\text{tr}} + \text{DO} + \text{IO}: \text{Prep}_{\text{io}} + \text{Nominal} + x'' \rightarrow$
Source string

A friend wrote	a letter to John
Subj $x' + V_{\text{tr}}$	DO IO

$x + \text{Subj}': \text{Nominal} + x' + V_{\text{pass}} + \text{-Marker}_{\text{past part}} + V_{\text{tr}} +$
$\text{DO} + (\text{Prep}_{\text{agent}} + \text{Agent}: \text{Subj})$
Resulting string

John was	written	a letter
Subj' $x' + V_{\text{pass}}$	$\text{-Marker}_{\text{past part}} + V_{\text{tr}}$	DO

(by   a friend)
Prep$_{\text{agent}}$ Agent

This example of the passive transformation was chosen to show in a general way how deep structure can be formulated in a common-core transformational grammar.

Now we shall see how the interrogative transformation may be treated in a Portuguese–English grammar, and how the interrogatives may be the direct object of certain verbs. It may be of interest to note that English interrogatives must undergo obligatory changes for stand-alone function (i.e., as direct questions), while Portuguese interrogatives do not necessarily need changes.

2. Interrogative Direct Object (Portuguese–English)

2.1 $x + \text{Subj} + x' + V_{\text{tr}} + \text{DO} + x'' \rightarrow$
Source strings

He	wants	the book
Subj	$x' + V_{tr}$	DO
Êle	quer	o livro
Subj	$x' + V_{tr}$	DO

$x + \text{Interrog}_{\text{inanimate}} + \text{Subj} + x' + V_{tr} + x''$

2.2 $\text{Interrog}_{\text{inanimate}} \rightarrow \begin{cases} \text{(E) Interrog}_{\text{inanimate}} \\ \text{(P) Interrog}_{\text{inanimate}} \end{cases}$

2.2.1E   (E) $\text{Interrog}_{\text{inanimate}} \rightarrow \underline{\text{what}}$

2.2.1P   (P) $\text{Interrog}_{\text{inanimate}} \rightarrow \underline{\text{o que}}$
Resulting strings

What	he	wants
$\text{Interrog}_{\text{inanimate}}$	Subj	$x' + V_{tr}$
O que	êle	quer
$\text{Interrog}_{\text{inanimate}}$	Subj	$x' + V_{tr}$

These strings may serve as the direct object in English and Portuguese sentences of the kind that follow:

I know what he wants
        Interrogative string

Eu sei o que êle quer
        Interrogative string

The Portuguese interrogative string may stand as it is as a direct question, but the English string must be operated on by the following rule:

     Obligatory Rule for a Direct Question

2.2.2E $x + \text{(E) Interrog}_{\text{inanimate}} + \text{Subj} + x' + V_{tr} + x'' \rightarrow$
Source string

What	he	wants
$\text{Interrog}_{\text{inanimate}}$	Subj	$x' + V_{tr}$

$x + \text{(E) Interrog}_{\text{inanimate}} + x' + V_{\text{interrog}} + \text{Subj} + V_{tr}$

2.2.3E $V_{\text{interrog}} \rightarrow \underline{\text{do}}$
Resulting string

What	does	he	want
$\text{Interrog}_{\text{inanimate}}$	$x' + V_{\text{interrog}}$	Subj	V_{tr}

Optional

2.2.2P　$x + \underline{\text{o que}} + \text{Subj} + x' + V_{tr} + x'' \rightarrow$

Source string

O que êle　　quer
　$\underline{}$　Subj　$x' + V_{tr}$

$$x + \begin{Bmatrix} \underline{\text{o que}} \\ \underline{\text{que}} \\ \underline{\text{que é que}} \end{Bmatrix} + \text{Subj} + x' + V_{tr}$$

Resulting strings

O que êle　　quer
　$\underline{}$　Subj　$x' + V_{tr}$

Que êle　　quer
　$\underline{}$　Subj　$x' + V_{tr}$

Que é que êle　　quer
　$\underline{}$　Subj　$x' + V_{tr}$

Sentence elements other than the direct object may be interrogated by means of other similar transformations to produce such sentences as in English:

I wonder who he is.
I wonder when he will arrive.
I wonder where he is.
I wonder how he is.
I wonder to whom he is speaking.
I wonder why he does that.

Next, consideration will be given to an accounting for the imperative in English and Spanish. The starting point is with a class of factive nominals serving as direct objects of verbs expressing wishes or commands.

3. Imperative (Spanish–English)

Let x and its primes equal any other elements or null in the sentence in which the factive nominal is included. Let y and its primes equal any other elements in the factive nominal occurring after the subject. x' includes first person and present tense markers. y or its primes include second person markers.

3.1　$x + \text{Subj} + x' + V_{tr_{imper}} + \text{DO: Introducer} + \text{Subj}' + y + x'' \rightarrow$
　　Source strings

I　　desire　　　that　　　you　　go
Subj　$x' + V_{tr_{imper}}$　　Introducer　Subj'　y

Yo   deseo   que   usted salga
Subj $x' + V_{\text{trimper}}$ Introducer   Subj' y
(Subj') y
Resulting strings
(You)   go
Subj' y
(Usted)   salga
Subj' y

3.1.1S   Subj' $+ y \rightarrow y +$ Subj'
Resulting string
Salga usted

Non-negative Spanish imperatives with object pronouns preceding the conjugated verb must be transformed as follows:

3.1.2S $y +$ Pronoun(s) $+ y' +$ Verbal Phrase$_{\text{last element}} + y'' \rightarrow$
Source strings
Se   la   escriba
Pronoun$_{\text{io}}$ Pronoun$_{\text{do}}$ Verbal Phrase$_{\text{last element}}$
'Write it to him'
Se   la   trate de escribir
Pronoun$_{\text{io}}$ Pronoun$_{\text{do}}$ y' Verb Phrase $_{\text{last element}}$
'Try to write it to him'
$y' +$ Verbal Phrase$_{\text{last element}} +$ Pronoun(s) $+ y''$
Resulting strings
Escriba   se   la
Verbal Phrase$_{\text{last element}}$ Pronoun$_{\text{io}}$ Pronoun$_{\text{do}}$
Trate de escribir   se   la
y' Verbal Phrase$_{\text{last element}}$ Pronoun$_{\text{io}}$ Pronoun$_{\text{do}}$

In writing, the last verbal element and pronouns would be written as one word and a written stress would appear, producing *Escríbasela* and *Trate de escribírsela*.

Upon careful examination of one particular transformational grammar of English, the writer took exception to the justification offered by the author[1] for a number of points of analysis. After having been steeped in the details of Spanish–English and Portuguese–English grammar, it seemed to the writer that the English transformational grammar often resorted to

---

[1] Robert B. Lees, 'The Grammar of English Nominalizations', *International Journal of American Linguistics*, XXVI, 3, part 2. Publication 12 of the Indiana University Research Center in Anthropology, Folklore, and Linguistics, 1960.

arbitrary decisions, or weak or erroneous justification. Of course, these thoughts were in the context of contrastive grammar. The writer is not suggesting that there is 'a correct' analysis.

Several points where the writer differs with R. B. Lees in his analysis of English[1] include the imperative (already discussed here and viewed by Lees as generated by phrase structure), the labeling of certain relative clauses as question-word clauses as answering questions, and numerous source strings for nominalizations.

The point expressed here is that if there are language universals, and it is presumed that there are at least some, they will not be revealed except accidentally by basing all justification for decisions of analysis on the data displayed by a single language. For single-language description, there can be no quarrel with basing all decisions on the convenience offered by the data. For contrastive analysis, it seems apparent that pressures are exerted from each language base. The writer suggests that the common core transformational grammar elaborating on Harris'[2] concepts of transfer grammar offers a convenient means of dealing with these pressures from opposite directions. The common core consists of the broadest possible generalizations based on the data offered by two languages. When generalization is not feasible, appended single language rules apply.

Even broader generalizations might be made for more than two languages in the form of a common core. If the common core is general enough to encompass several or a number of languages, the statements in the common core express sub-universals, at least, if not universals. Even the appended rules might be ordered and arranged to apply to more than one language.

In theory, the writer believes that a universal grammar might take the shape of the kind of contrastive grammar discussed here.

---

[1] *Ibid.*   [2] Harris, 'Transfer grammar'.

On the adequacy of phonological theories for contrastive studies

K. KOHLER

Contrastive studies have long been a well-established field of research within modern descriptive linguistics. Their aim is clear: they are to provide separate detailed phonological and syntactic analyses of different languages according to the principles of structural linguistics and to show up the differences and similarities by comparing the results. Studies of this kind have never been a mere intellectual game of professional linguists, but have always been produced with a clear practical purpose, namely with a view to their application in language teaching. The Contrastive Structure Series edited by the Center for Applied Linguistics bears ample witness to this approach.

The idea behind it is to find a way of predicting those mistakes in pronunciation and in sentence construction which foreign learners of a language are likely to make and to devise drills to prevent these mistakes from occurring. The implication is that structural comparisons of the kind characterized here supply the key to language interference and consequently are a necessary prerequisite to predictive statements and subsequent methods of correction. The question is whether this claim is legitimate and can be substantiated or needs important modifications, and whether the particular contrastive studies we are familiar with are less the reflection of a linguistic reality, than the outcome of a particular view of language imposed by structural linguistic *theory* in such Saussurian terms as system, *langue*, *parole*. This paper follows up these questions and tries to determine, with regard to phonology, the adequacy and applicability of different theoretical approaches in contrastive studies.

No practically oriented human activity is devoid of theory, and practical structure comparisons for foreign language learning lean heavily on structuralist linguistic theory. In the field of so-called taxonomic phonology the concepts of such a theory are distinctive units, such as phonemes on the

[83]

one hand, and variants of these which can be covered by general statement on the other. Reliance on these concepts in contrastive studies leads to relating fundamental mistakes which interfere with intelligibility to such distinctive units, particularly to phonemes, and the less important deviations to allophonic variation. So contrastive phonologies based on the taxonomic principle aim at setting out phoneme systems, combinatorial possibilities of phonemes and non-distinctive variations of these units in different languages (the first aim being usually realized more fully than the other two), and at working out exercises that teach the student first and foremost those pronunciation phenomena that have been treated as distinctive contrasts. Dependence on linguistic theory could not be more obvious; this does not prejudge the adequacy and applicability of the particular view.

It can be said that on the whole this theoretical assumption works pretty well. If structural differences have been set up in terms of phonemes, allophones and phonotactics at any point between two languages then (1) the chances are extremely high that interference will occur in the learning process and (2) the interferences in distinctive units will be more serious with regard to intelligibility. Numerous examples can be cited here: English learners render German /x/ as /k/, French learners render German /ç/ as /ʃ/, Japanese or Chinese learners render /r/ in any language as /l/. None of these predictive statements has absolute validity, however. There are for instance no word initial /ʃ/-clusters, except /ʃr/, in English. And yet English speakers have no difficulty whatsoever in producing and auditorily discriminating the combinations /ʃp/, /ʃt/, /ʃm/, /ʃn/, /ʃl/, whereas the clusters /ts/ or /pt/ equally absent from English cause trouble and are usually replaced by 'simpler' sounds. 'Data-shmata, I like my theory' is a famous example. On the other hand, the non-occurrence of an opposition such as /y(:)/ : /i(:)/ in German may interfere very little with intelligibility (one reason presumably being, in this case, the existence of unrounded vowels instead of rounded ones in a number of German dialects so that speakers of German are familiar with them and can thus make allowances more easily). Non-distinctive features, however, such as vowel-length before voiced or voiceless consonants, can have a great influence. The connection of predictive statements in contrastive studies with elements of taxonomic phonological theory can thus only be a first approximation, and in many cases it will fail completely. Its adequacy and applicability is thus limited.

Another assumption that is usually made in this context is that phonological units are neutral as to articulation and auditory perception and could thus be given either auditory or articulatory labels or both, but are best described in articulatory terms because they are at present better defined and accessible. It follows from this hypothesis for contrastive studies that what is difficult to articulate is also difficult to hear. This is a totally unsubstantiated assumption. [б] is extremely troublesome to produce for most speakers, but very easy to detect. Similarly, [ʍeɬ] compared with [ŋɑl], or certain intonations and voice qualities may cause no problem of perception, but of articulation (in which connection it is irrelevant that the hearer may find it extremely difficult to *describe* what he distinguishes by ear). Contrariwise, the distinction between /tl/ and /kl/ is readily performed, but not easily heard. Differences in place of articulation seem to be least resistant to productive imitation; the manner of articulation, and glottal and pharyngal mechanisms are far more difficult to acquire; in perception the ordering seems to be reversed.

It is certainly true that in large areas degrees of difficulty in articulation and perception coincide and one may equate auditory and articulatory characterizations of such utterances *for practical purposes*, but certainly not in all cases, and there is no correspondence between the two in principle. Whereas articulation probably rests mainly on a segmental basis, nervous discharges as motor commands being discrete, auditory perception is probably largely non-segmental. Alliteration and other sound play in illiterate societies seems to suggest that certain segmental positions must be relevant in the auditory field as well. But in any case we do not need a motor theory of speech perception and therefore need make no assumption as to the preponderance of articulatory specifications of phonemes. The facts encountered in language learning speak against it. One might object that nonsense ear-training in general phonetics courses shows over and over again that students who have learnt to articulate certain sounds (or sequences) will also be better at detecting them aurally. But here previous articulation helps to introduce a segmental interpretation into an auditory impression (which happens in any acquisition of segmental writing and is required by an alphabetic transcription) since the speaker is at the same time a hearer and can thus associate certain articulations with certain auditory *Gestalten* in him and can use this association for the articulatory segmentation of other auditory preceptions. This is therefore no argument against the hypothesis of a basic difference between articulation and hearing; on the contrary it confirms it.

Moreover, scholars in contrastive linguistics usually work on the principle that there either is interference or there is not, according to the presence or absence of structural differences, and that consequently articulatory acquisition (or aural discrimination and identification) is either difficult or not. But ease of imitation (or recognition) of unfamiliar sound phenomena is certainly a graded scale. Whereas /ʃt-/ is easy, /pt-/ is difficult to articulate (or to hear) for English speakers, at the beginning of a word, /ft/ seems to take a position between the two. Naive speakers can still make it without too much effort and will easily recognize it, but they are less happy with it than with /ʃt/, as several informal enquiries have shown. This is a very interesting field that needs further investigation, separately for articulation and for perception, of course. A first step in this direction is the inspiring article by R. W. Brown and D. C. Hildum ('Expectancy and the perception of syllables', *Language* 32 (1956), 411 ff.).

Because of its failure (1) to predict mistakes and their gravity in all cases, (2) to distinguish between speaker and hearer explicitly, and (3) to explicate a grading of difficulties, taxonomic phonology cannot be regarded as an adequate theory for contrastive linguistics. It is only a first approximation procedure which can render valuable services, and further and more detailed practical contrastive studies with more phonetic information should be produced on this basis to indicate the *possible* areas of interference. But this is all it can do; reliable prediction of actual mistakes needs different information, which taxonomic phonology cannot provide.

The question therefore needs to be asked whether generative phonology could offer an improvement. It must be stressed that proper comparisons of the phonologies of different languages have not been provided in the generative camp, and even if they had been, they would not have been intended for practical application in language teaching. MIT linguistics is largely a-practical, in search of universal truths, as is summed up in this quotation from Chomsky: 'They [Bloch and Hockett] are considering rather the problems of gathering and organizing data, and thus their indirect argument for the conditions of biuniqueness and local determinacy at most shows that it would be convenient for the linguist if there were a level of representation meeting these conditions, but it does not bear on the question of the existence of this level as a part of linguistic structure.' ('Current issues in linguistic theory', in: Fodor and Katz, *Readings in the Philosophy of Language*, Englewood Cliffs, 1964, p. 108.)

The firm insistence on the ideal speaker-hearer precludes the necessary separation of production and perception. Prediction and grading of mistakes is not easier within the generative framework in spite of the elaborate marking conventions. So generative phonology shows no advantage over taxonomic phonemics in these respects. On the contrary, it fails at another point where taxonomic phonology is fairly adequate for contrastive studies, namely in the promiscuous mixing of levels. All morphophonological information (without regard to the productivity of the process) is worked into the lexicon and the resulting quasi-mystical underlying forms are said to have psychological reality. The distribution of [ŋ]'and [ŋg] in English and relations between words like *divine* and *divinity* are interesting facts, which must all be stated in a complete phonological description, and we should be grateful to Chomsky and Halle for pointing out correspondences of this sort, largely neglected by earlier generations, but it should be done in its proper place, in morphophonology, not in phonological representations in the lexicon. *King* cannot contain [g] in any sense of 'psychological reality', unless it is influenced by the spelling; the motor commands are the ones for [kiŋ], not for [kiŋg] with subsequent deletion of [g]. Similarly the articulation controlled in *divinity* is [i], not underlying [ai].

To account for linguistic interference we have to know the rules of articulatory movement control, which cannot possibly be expressed in pseudo-psychological forms that are determined by historical alternations of different degrees of petrification. This kind of morphophonology makes any meaningful comparison of the articulatory behaviour of speakers of different languages impossible. Taxonomic phonology, although still far from the goal, was more adequate at this point.

I am, of course, not advocating a return to a complete separation of levels of taxonomic *theory*, which tried to exclude meaning altogether and asked pointless questions, e.g. about the phonemic status of [x] and [ç] in German. Taxonomic *practice*, particularly in contrastive studies, has always recognized word and morpheme boundaries, and that is all the morphological information necessary for an adequate phonology. Phonology is the level of articulatory control and auditory perception in all its gradations. Phonological alternations belong to a separate level of morphophonology, and different degrees of productivity of these correspondences must be distinguished, the complexity of which was treated in great detail by Baudouin de Courtenay 75 years ago!

It may also be suggested that the MIT concept of redundancy is just as inflated as the concept of phonology. Although [s] in English *stone* is fully determined in the sense that there is no English word beginning with a consonant other than [s] before [t], yet it is not the only possible consonant in strictly articulatory, lexicon-independent, terms. English speakers can produce (and recognize) other consonants. This kind of lexical redundancy is clearly different from the redundancy of palatality in English *king* induced by articulatory control.

To put contrastive studies and their practical application in language teaching on a better foundation than taxonomic phonology we cannot substitute generative phonology, we do not need an ideal speaker-hearer, but a real speaker *and* a real hearer. And to achieve this linguists need the help of psychologists; purely linguistic operations can only give a necessary and very useful first approximation; for further work the concepts of phoneme, phonological system, *langue, parole* can only be a hindrance.

The predictability of interference phenomena in the English speech of native speakers of Hungarian

WILLIAM NEMSER

The experimental study to be discussed was designed to test certain basic theoretical concepts underlying contrastive linguistics. The investigation was conceived as optimally favorable to these concepts since it deals with the contact of phonological systems, presumably the most rigidly structured aspects of language, and insulates these systems, as far as possible, from the influence of higher-order linguistic and extralinguistic factors.

The relevant concepts, as stated or implied in theoretical studies by such scholars as Uriel Weinreich and Einar Haugen, following earlier work by Boas, Polivanov, Trubetzkoy and others, are:

(1) Differences between the bilingual's primary (native) and secondary (target) language will result in interference, i.e. deviations from the norm of the latter system.

(2) The interference results from the identification of secondary system elements with those of the primary system.

(3) Patterns of identification, and hence interference, are regular.

(4) Perceptual and productive interference patterns are similar.

(5) These patterns are predictable on the basis of contrastive (or 'dialinguistic') analysis, i.e. a comparison of descriptions of the phonological systems of the languages in contact.

The study under discussion attempted to test these concepts by reference to the perception and production of English stops and interdental fricatives ($/\theta/$ and $/\eth/$, as in *thank* and *that*, or *bath*, and *bathe*) by native speakers of Hungarian having a limited knowledge of English.

Dialinguistic analysis

A contrastive analysis of the stop subsystems of Hungarian and English reveals the following differences:

(1) Hungarian homorganic pairs are opposed through voicing, English pairs through the tense-lax feature.

(2) Labial, apical and dorsal pairs occur in both languages, but the Hungarian system also includes two palatal stops, /t'/ and /d'/, which are opposed to the other lingual stops through spread-tongue articulation.

(3) Hungarian voiceless stops are unaspirated, while in English aspiration plays a crucial role in the identification of tense stops in initial position, medially before stressed vowels, and sometimes finally.[1]

(4) Hungarian voiceless stops are redundantly tense, and Hungarian voiced stops redundantly lax; English tense stops are voiceless, but English lax stops are frequently partially or totally unvoiced, especially in final position.

Unlike the English stops, the English interdentals have no counterparts in Hungarian sharing their modal and local characteristics. However their locus feature is shared by the Hungarian stops, and their friction type by the Hungarian labial fricatives. Hungarian sibilants share both friction and locus with the interdentals, but contrast in friction *type* as high to low intensity and frequency.[2]

In sum, since modal and local features play similar roles in the stop subsystems of Hungarian and English (apart from the non-distinctive aspiration feature), the problem of the interpretation of English stops by Hungarians concerns the tense-lax feature. Since Hungarian voiceless stops are phonetically tense, and Hungarian voiced stops are phonetically lax, the problem is not one of feature *generation* but of feature *function*.

The English interdentals, on the other hand, while also opposed through the tense-lax feature, face Hungarian speakers with the added problem of feature *distribution* since the modal and local features of low-intensity friction and apicality do not co-occur in Hungarian.

Phonemic distributional rules for stops are, in general, more restrictive in Hungarian than in English, with fewer cluster types occurring and shared clusters having lower lexical and textual frequencies.

[1] See John Lotz, Louis Gerstman, Frances Ingemann, Arthur S. Abramson and William Nemser, 'The perception of English stops by speakers of English, Spanish, Hungarian and Thai; a tape-cutting experiment', *Language and Speech* III (1960), 71–7.

[2] See Katherine Harris, 'Cues for the discrimination of American-English fricatives in spoken syllables', *Language and Speech* I (1958), 1–7; Peter Strevens, 'Spectra of fricative noise in human speech', *Language and Speech* III (1960), 32–49.

The problem facing the Hungarian interpreter of the English interdentals is, of course, one in *total* distribution. The most relevant information relates the distribution of the interdentals to that of the Hungarian phonemes paradigmatically most similar to them: the labial fricatives, apical stops and sibilants.

Predictions

The *predictions* yielded by the contrastive analysis just presented are:

(1) English tense stops will be regularly identified with their Hungarian voiceless counterparts (perhaps as examples of covert interference).

(2) Voiced allophones of English lax stops will be identified with the corresponding Hungarian voiced stops, but

(3) *Voiceless* allophones of English lax stops will often be identified with Hungarian *voiceless* stops.

(4) Interpretations of the English interdentals as labial fricatives, apical stops or groove sibilants are, in general, equally likely except in contexts where distributional rules favor one or another choice.

Alternate dialinguistic analyses

The contrastive analysis employed above differs in certain respects from those based on other current theories of phonologic structure. The International Phonetic Association framework, since it posits no internal organization among phonologic units, can furnish little information on similarities or differences among phonologic units in the same or different systems, and hence lacks predictive power. On the other hand, such structurally conceived formulations as those of Roman Jakobson and André Martinet take no account of recent advances in phonetic analysis revealing marked differences between sibilant and non-sibilant friction types: with the special acoustic qualities noted above, the sibilants are perceptually characterized by an independence of context.[1]

The phonetic approach advocated by Haugen would favor the assignment of English tense (voiceless) stops to their Hungarian voiceless (tense) counterparts, but prediction of the assignment of voiceless allophones of English lax stops poses a problem since the two features of voicelessness and laxness suggest different solutions, and voiceless occurrences of the

[1] Harris, 'The discrimination of American-English fricatives'. Jakobson, for example, opposes labial and interdental fricatives (strident vs. mellow), and groups labials and sibilants (as strident).

lax interdental suggest no fewer than six interpretations: as Hungarian /d/, /t/, /z/, /s/, /v/, or /f/.

Martinet's serial pattern, with labials, apicals, palatals, sibilants, affricates and velars all constituting orders, on the whole suggests the assignment of the interdentals to the labial fricatives or apical stops, rather than to the sibilants, in light of a 'hole in the pattern' in the palatal order between the position into which the interdentals fall and the sibilants:

p/b	t/d	t'/d'	c/ʒ	č/ǯ	k/g
f/v	θ/ð		s/z	š/ž	

Jakobson's binary framework posits an unequivocal affinity between the English interdentals and the Hungarian groove sibilants. These sets share three features: non-compactness (dominant back cavity), acuteness (medial constriction), and continuancy, and are opposed only redundantly as mellow (simple impediment) to strident (complex impediment).

The more recent formulation by Noam Chomsky and Morris Halle[1] differs in few relevant respects from Jakobson's. Their new 'anterior' category (obstruction in front of the palatal-alveolar region) is here equatable with non-compact, and their new 'coronal' category (raised tongue front) partially so with acute. However the apical and palatal stops, grouped together as acute by Jakobson, are opposed in the Chomsky–Halle formulation as coronal (raised *front*) to non-coronal (raised *body*), while special affinities now unite the palatals and dorsals as both non-coronal and non-anterior.

Testing procedures

A series of pilot tests roughly localized the area of the Hungarian phonologic system involved in the interpretation of the English stops and interdentals – in the case of the latter phonemes, the three Hungarian sets, the labial fricatives, apical stops and groove sibilants all apparently did play a role. These pilot tests also established the feasibility of the testing techniques.

Six full-scale tests, of from 222 to 576 items, were designed. They included measures of ability to perceive, to produce and to repeat items containing the test phonemes.

Oddball and transcription procedures were used on the perception tests

[1] *The Sound Pattern of English*, New York, 1969, pp. 304, 306–8.

(in the former type the informant tries to designate the deviant one of four stimuli, e.g., *tin, thin, tin, tin*).

Productions of English stops were elicited when informants repeated recorded nonsense syllables with the addition, in initial or final position, of a stop (or control phoneme) represented by a symbol on their scripts (thus if they heard [is] and saw *t* on their scripts they would say [tis]).

Renditions of the English interdentals were elicited when informants retranslated the Hungarian equivalents for common English words containing the interdentals in what they were told was a vocabulary test.

On the repetition test, informants attempted to imitate syllables containing test phonemes or control stimuli.

The same test items (unrecognized) were used on the 'Hungarian-ear Test' in which informants were instructed to force an interpretation of English sounds in terms of Hungarian phonemic categories, transcribing the test items in Hungarian orthography.

Finally, the 'Spill-bill Test' sought judgments of post-initial stops after the removal, by tape-cutting, of a preceding sibilant. The same test in an earlier study had revealed a clear tendency among English speakers to identify these residual segments as lax.[1]

To inhibit the intrusion of higher-order (lexical, grammatical, morphophonemic) interference, English nonsense syllables were used on all tests except the retranslation and residual-stop tests, and polysyllabic items only on the former.

Contexts for test phonemes were chosen on the basis of typicality in English. The basic test-item form of test phoneme plus test context was elaborated only where the sequence as it stood violated English rules (e.g. [θɹ], [ðɛ]), or where it was meaningful in English.[2]

Perception and repetition tests were recorded on magnetic tape by native speakers of English. Samples were administered to other native speakers to establish the viability, on the recordings, of the distinctions being tested.

Subjects

Eleven speakers of Standard Hungarian, all with a very limited knowledge of English, served as subjects. The study was conceived as an examination in depth of a restricted set of problems with a small group of subjects. On most tests, the subject group was limited to from four to six informants.

Most tests required between one and two hours to administer, but sessions included frequent rest periods.

[1] See Lotz *et al.*, 'The perception of English stops'.
[2] Again, the latter restriction did not apply to the Spill-bill and Retranslation tests.

Results

Responses showed definite regularities, with general consistency for individual informants and agreement among informants. However, considerable qualitative and quantitative variation in interference patterns was also characteristic of the data.

In most general terms, when errors occurred the interdentals were:

(*a*) usually *perceived* as labial fricatives:

	T	S	F
%	10	10	80

(where figures are rounded to the nearest ten, and where [θ] and [ð] results are pooled);

(*b*) they are almost always *produced* as apical stops, and *never* as labial fricatives:

	T	S	F
%	90	10	0

(*c*) the English *tense* interdental was imitated as either a sibilant, fricative or stop, in that order of preference:

	t	s	f
%	10	50	40

(*d*) but imitative interpretations of the *lax* interdental showed the reverse order of preference:

	d	z	v
%	50	10	40

(*e*) A considerable number of the productive and imitative responses were phone blends or sequences, often not identifiable with phoneme categories in either Hungarian or English: [sθ], [td], [fs], [tθ], [ts], [st]. *Perceptual* blends were apparently also frequent since responses often indicated that the interdentals were heard as neither totally distinct from, nor identical with familiar Hungarian phonemes.

(*f*) The interpretation of the stops was far more uniform. Members of English homorganic pairs were almost invariably identified with the corresponding Hungarian phonemes on all tests, in the case of the lax stops with total disregard of the voicing factor.

(*g*) In the production of the tense stops, aspiration errors were very numerous. With underaspiration, deviations included apparent phonemicization of the spirant element, affrication, and other types of distortion.

(*h*) The results of the residual-stop test showed that, unlike English speakers, the subjects usually identified these residual elements with English *tense* stops.

(*i*) On the 'Hungarian-ear' test the results for the interdental resembled those of the repetition test; however the 'error' rates for the stops (i.e. assignment to the non-analogous Hungarian category) were actually lower.

(*j*) On perception and repetition tests, when errors occurred in the interpretation of stop *loci*, they were never interpreted as palatals.

Implications

The test results imply serious shortcomings in the theoretical concepts validated, at least as they apply to language learning, and even raise questions relevant to general linguistic theory:

(1) Patterns of association established by learners between phoneme categories of the languages in contact are far less stable and more complex than has been assumed.

(2) Contact theory, by suggesting that only the categories of the languages in contact are available to the learner, fails to account for the variety and frequency of phoneme blends assignable to neither system.

(3) Neither the theory of language contact nor general linguistic theory can accommodate the apparent independence of the perceptual and productive modalities in the interpretation of alien phonemes.

(4) Different phonemic theories yield different predictions; no theory, including that employed in the study, predicts or accounts for interference patterns as complex as those resulting from the contact of the Hungarian and English phonemic systems, even where the influence of higher-order linguistic factors is minimized.

(5) Predictions are often too vague to be useful. Only the Jakobsonian-based formulations yielded explicit predictions, and they were generally erroneous.

(6) Formulations positing a close relationship between palatal stops and other lingual stops, those of Martinet, Jakobson and Chomsky and Halle, received no support from the test results, despite the fact that locus confusions were not rare.

(7) Notions of symmetrical patterning received some support from parallel interpretations of the interdentals on the perception and production tests, but on the repetition test interpretations of the two phonemes differ radically.

(8) Comparisons of the distributional rules in the two languages favored as many *in*correct as correct predictions, and error rates were as high in familiar as in unfamiliar contexts.

(9) Error rates were far lower than anticipated. Even the subject whose knowledge of English was most rudimentary, one whose productive system did not include the interdentals, usually perceived these phonemes as distinct from any Hungarian phonemes.

(10) Finally, the extremely low error rate in the interpretation of English stops, and its lack of correlation with voicing characteristics of the English models, suggests that a reappraisal of the tense-lax and voiced-voiceless features in the two languages, and perhaps in other languages as well, might reveal unexpected similarities between the two categories.

Clearly validation studies must remain an intrinsic part of contrastive linguistics for some time to come. At present they are clearly a prerequisite for the successful application of contrastive linguistics to language pedagogy. Such research is equally required for the theoretical development of contrastive linguistics, and may prove valuable for general linguistic theory as well.

Sentence complexity in contrastive linguistics

G. R. KRESS

This paper is in two parts. The first gives a brief review of the subject of sentence complexity, while the second attempts to point out some possible applications of the subject in contrastive studies. The major statements on the subject are contained in V. H. Yngve, 'A model and an hypothesis for language structure',[1] and G. A. Miller and N. A. Chomsky, 'Finitary models of language users'.[2] A recently published book by I. M. Schlesinger[3] deals with the same problem. Although there appear to be useful applications, there has been little reflection of this discussion in language teaching practice.

In a recent article on 'Contrastive linguistics and language teaching'[4] Nickel and Wagner divide the domain of foreign language instruction into two components. One is concerned with the description of grammars G and G^1 and determines which rules of the new grammar G^1 are to be taught. This they call the didactic component. The other determines the manner in which the new rules are to be taught and learned. This they call the methodic component. The application of sentence complexity is a matter for the methodic component. In other words a grammatical description of the languages is presupposed, and the interest is with the device D which uses this description for the production and understanding of sentences.

The division into passive and active language ability is generally useful and widely employed, though the terms active and passive are somewhat misleading. It seems preferable to refer to a device utilized by the speaker/

---

[1] V. H. Yngve, 'A model and an hypothesis for language structure', *Proceedings of the American Philosophical Society*, vol. 104, No. 5, October 1960.

[2] In R. D. Luce, R. R. Bush and E. Galanter, eds., *Handbook of Mathematical Psychology*, vol. II, ch. 13. New York, Wiley, 1963.

[3] I. M. Schlesinger, *Sentence Structure and the Reading Process*, Janua Linguarium, series minor, 69, Mouton, The Hague.

[4] G. Nickel and K-H. Wagner, 'Contrastive linguistics and language teaching', *IRAL*, vol. 1/3, August 1968.

writer on the one hand, and the listener/reader on the other. An over-simplified version of this device for the listener might look like this: the device D recognizes sentences by producing simultaneously or after a short lapse of time a sentence like the one it has received. To do this it utilizes a grammar G which contains the rules for producing this sentence. In the case of the learner of a language, G may not contain rules for producing a matching sentence, and there will be no or only partial understanding of the signal received.

Apart from this obvious limitation to understanding other limitations operate. They are due to the finiteness of the device, that is, due to the fact that memory is fixed. As pointed out by Chomsky and Miller there is an important distinction between a device with a limited memory storing a grammar G, which, due to the finiteness of its (short-term) memory can assign structural descriptions only to a limited set S^1 of sentences generated by G, and a device designed to understand only S^1. The analogy used by Chomsky and Miller to illustrate this point is of a person knowing the rules of multiplication but prevented by memory limitations from carrying out a multiplication of say, $2,485 \times 14,867$ in his head, and another person knowing only his tables up to 10. The former, given proper aids, such as pencil and paper, will be able to perform the required multiplication, the latter would have to be given additional instruction. The native speaker is in the former's position, the learner of a language in the latter's.

The grammar G is thus capable of producing sentences which exceed the memory limitations of the device. Whenever this happens one or more of a number of syntactic devices are likely to be involved. Yngve's depth hypothesis assumes that D is divided into a long-term and a short-term memory. The long-term memory stores the rules of G, while the short-term memory stores the unexpanded constituents of a PS rule. Due to its finiteness the short-term memory can store only a limited number of symbols (assumed to be 7 ± 2). The depth of a sentence is then equivalent to the largest number of unexpanded symbols held in the short-term memory at any one time during the production of a given sentence. The greater the depth of the sentence therefore, the closer the number of symbols held in the short-term memory is to exceeding the limitations of it. If the number of symbols to be expanded exceeds the limitation of the short-term memory the sentence cannot be produced. Thus the measure of depth is one indication of complexity.

It should be pointed out that lexical, semantic, and contextual considerations are not considered as contributing to sentence complexity in the sense here intended. To take a simple example, the sentences:

(1) Protozoen mit konstanter Körperform besitzen meist monaxone Formen, welche ihnen eine Polarität verleiht

and

(2) Bohnenkaffee mit viel Schlagsahne hat ein herrliches Aroma, das ihm weite Beliebtheit gibt

are considered as being of the same complexity.

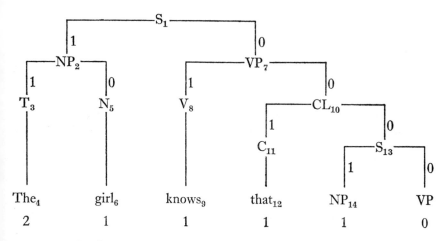

Depth: 2; Mean depth $d = 1$
Structural complexity (node to terminal node ratio): $15/6 = 2\cdot5$

Embedding is a common syntactic feature which can lead to an overloading of the short-term memory. However, in the case of embedding it is not unlikely that extra-syntactic means are utilized to aid understanding. In the case of

(3) This is the hole, that the rat, which the cat, whom the dog bit, caught, made

the syntactic dependencies between items can be altered, yet the interpretation will remain the same

(4) This is the hole, that the cat, which the rat, whom the dog bit, made, caught.

It seems very likely that in the case of nested constructions knowledge about the external world, about rats and holes, cats and dogs, is used to help in understanding. In other words, although the device may not assign a syntactic description to the sentence, there are other components of the device which assign a meaning to the sentence. If the content of the sentence is neutralized this extra-syntactic component fails to operate.

(5) This is the boy, that the lad, whom the child, which our friend saw, knows, hit.

Another phenomenon which contributes to sentence complexity, and which has received quite a lot of attention, is transformational complexity. The names of G. A. Miller,[1] J. Mehler,[2] and T. G. Bever[3] are prominent in the research conducted in this field. The work proceeds from the assumption that the syntactic information contained in a sentence is processed by the device in two parts: as information about the Kernel, and as additional information about the optional transformations the Kernel has undergone, which is stored in the form of transformational tags. The greater the transformational remove from the Kernel, the more information has to be stored in the short-term memory, and consequently, the greater the complexity of the sentence. There are two points about this assumption. (1) The theoretical status of the concept Kernel sentence has been questioned. Later work (such as Mehler and Bever, 1968) takes account of this and relates transformational complexity to the deep structure of a sentence. Complexity is seen as directly related to the derivational history of the sentence, or, specifically to the number of deep-structure sentences underlying a sentence. As the authors of the paper point out, the notion of deep structure is becoming increasingly abstract. Bach and Harms[4] cite a derivation of 'Floyd broke the glass' which is composed of eight underlying sentences of which they give the following paraphrase: I declare to you that it past that it happen that Floyd do cause it to come about that it BE the glass broken. (2) There may be independently variable factors involved in transformational complexity. The negation transformation causes greater perceptual difficulty to the device than the question transformation, due possibly to psychological factors quite outside the realm of syntax.[5]

There are several other indices of complexity. Structural complexity measures the amount of computation performed by the device in generating a sentence, and it is expressed as the ratio of total number of nodes in the

[1] G. A. Miller, 'Some psychological studies of grammar', *American Psychology* (1962), 17: 784–62.

[2] J. Mehler, 'Some effects of grammatical transformations in the recall of English sentences' *JVLB* (1963), 2: 346–51.

[3] T. G. Bever, and J. Mehler 'Sentences can be memorized in terms of their basic syntactic structure', *PEGS Paper*, No. 39, 31 May, 1968.

[4] E. Bach and R. T. Harms, eds., *Universals in Linguistic Theory*, New York, Holt, Rinehart and Winston, 1968.

[5] P. C. Wason, 'Psychological Aspects of Negation', *Communication Research Centre Papers*, Paper II, University College, London, 1962.

PS tree to the number of terminal nodes in the derivation. Sentence length, number of syllables per sentence, are two more indices which are frequently mentioned.

These syntactic characteristics can be used to devise means of grading sentences according to their syntactic complexity. An index can be assigned to a sentence indicating the mean depth by adding the depths of the terminal items and dividing by the number of terminal nodes. Similarly, indices indicating degree of nesting, self-embedding or transformational complexity could be assigned to the sentence. Weightings would have to be given to the different indices, indicating their contribution to the overall complexity. For instance, transformations involving one step from the Kernel cause varying degrees of difficulty to the perceptual device (measured in terms of correct recall). In this way one could arrive at an average index which indicated the complexity of the sentence in terms of the criteria judged relevant. One would thus have an objective method of assessing the relative complexity of a sentence. Moreover, where the teacher is attempting to extend the learner's grammar by introducing new rules in his teaching materials it would seem useful to bear in mind the load imposed on the device by the various types of complexity mentioned.

It seems possible that certain types of complexity vary from language to language. The degree of left or right-branching seems to be a variable between languages, with languages such as Japanese or Turkish employing left-branching, English on the other hand, tending towards right-branching. Other types of complexity might also be language dependent. It is interesting to speculate whether D of a right-branching language differs in any respect from D^1 of a left-branching language. Errors in translations from German to English suggest that the device might at least be conditioned to work in a given way. Though German is not a left-branching language, it employs regressive constructions more frequently and readily than English. The following are a few modified noun-phrases from pp. 98–102, Helmut Heiber, *Die Republik von Weimar*, Munich 1966:

(6) ...das in jeder Hinsicht folgenschwerste Ergebnis der Inflation....

(7) ...jene an sich nicht nur inflationssicheren, sondern sogar – wie bei dem größten Teil der Landwirtschaft – durch die Möglichkeiten billiger Entschuldung inflationsbegünstigten Werte...

(8) ...die von der Rücksicht auf die Inflationsangst bestimmte Unzulänglichkeit der Abwehrmaßnahmen,...

(9) ...diese vom verlorenen Krieg verursachte inflatorische Entwicklung...

(10) Die nahezu steuerfrei und trotz Lohnerhöhungen mit relativ billiger, durch den ständigen Geldverfall um einen Teil ihres Lohns gebrachter Arbeitskraft produzierende Industrie...

In a reading improvement programme the aim is to increase facility in reading in the most efficient way possible. One of the important factors involved in the reading process is the assigning of structural descriptions to the sentences. By grading sentences according to syntactic complexity one can ensure that (a) the device is never overloaded; (b) language variable complexities are introduced in a controlled manner, so that, for instance, the English reader of German will gradually become used to dealing with a greater amount of left-branching; (c) working always from that which is known to that which is newer at one remove, new rules can be introduced without causing any of the time-consuming checks which occur when structures of too great a complexity are met. Thus the reader is always reading at full stretch, so to speak, while at the same time the rules contained in his grammar G^1 are being extended and he gradually becomes more familiar with more complex structures.

Comparative analysis of English and Czech phonology and prediction of errors in learning

VLADIMIR MACH

The contact of two languages may take place in the process of language learning or teaching or under other circumstances. In considering relevant aspects of language teaching and preparing adequate teaching materials this contact and the resulting interference of the native language with the target language cannot be ignored. Psychological research into the process of learning shows that one main task of a foreign language teacher should be to suppress the inhibitory effects of the native language on the internalization of the target language system. In this paper I would like to summarize experience gained in an attempt to put these principles into effect when devising more effective methods and materials for teaching the English spoken in Britain to Czech native speakers.

In classifying the different cases of interference we may proceed either on the basis of their results or on the basis of their origins.

Classification on the basis of results is useful in placing errors in a hierarchy of importance. But in each case we must distinguish between interference causing errors in perception and that causing errors in production. The latter may be of two kinds: those giving the pronunciation a 'foreign accent' (usually due to a wrong phonetic realization) and those changing the meaning of the speech. I consider the errors in perception as more serious than either of the other two.

In classifying interference according to its origin we find the following types:

(1) Difference in the system of phonological distinctions, when a correlation in the target language has no equivalent in the native language. This results in a failure to differentiate between the two phonemes of the target language (underdifferentiation), or in the identification of any of the two

phonemes either with one of the partners of the correlation or by a phoneme existing in the native language but phonetically different from either of the two phonemes of the correlation. An example of the former case is the identification of any member of the English correlation d – ð with d which is the only member of the correlation in the Czech system of consonants. An example of the latter case is the substitution of any member of the correlation e – æ by the lower-mid-front vowel ε.

(2) Differences in the combinatorial patterns of corresponding phonemes in the native language and the target language. As a result the learner either has difficulty in perceiving and producing a particular combination of phonemes or inserts a superfluous sound between the phonemes that do not combine in the native language. For example the sound ŋ, which is an allophone of n in Czech occurs only before k and g in the native language, while in the target language it occurs also finally and before a vowel. Consequently, while its pronunciation is perfectly easy for native Czech speakers when it occurs in English before k or g, it presents considerable difficulties finally and before a vowel, a g being wrongly inserted after ŋ in such words as sing or singing.

(3) Difference in the rules of neutralization. The resulting errors are either a transfer of neutralization from the native language into the target language, which is underdifferentiation (in the case of neutralization existing in the native language and not existing in the target language); or a failure to neutralize which is overdifferentiation (in the case of neutralization existing in the target language and not existing in the native language). An example of the former case is the neutralization of voice in final consonants in Czech so that only voiceless consonants can occur finally. This neutralization does not exist in English, so that without adequate training native Czech speakers can neither hear nor produce the difference between such words as hat – had, live – life, bits – bids. (Good information and exercise of the different vowel length before voiced and voiceless consonants can also help to remove this error.) As an example of the latter case may be given the neutralization of the distinction iː – iə before r in English, where only iə is possible. As no similar neutralization exists in Czech a common error of Czech native speakers is the pronunciation iː although the phoneme iə may be correctly pronounced by the same speakers in other positions.

(4) Difference in the phonetic realization of the allophones of the corresponding phonemes and difference in the positional variants. This may result in wrong perception of some phonemes through confusion with others, as well as wrong pronunciation. Thus Czech native speakers very often confuse the English r with w, or the combination tr with č in percep-

tion; and the English aspirated positional variants of the voiceless stops p, t, k are pronounced without aspiration as there are no such variants in Czech.

(5) Difference in non-segmental or suprasegmental or prosodic patterns. Serious interference from Czech as native language is caused by different rhythmic patterns. While in Czech the rhythm unit is the syllable, in English it is formed usually of a group of syllables of unequal length with the stressed one in various positions. The interference from the Czech rhythmic pattern causes both difficulties in understanding English native speakers and difficulties in the production of speech without a marked foreign accent. Intonation, important as it may be for the whole process of communication by speech, causes fewer difficulties from the interference of Czech as native language. Most of the intonational patterns in non-emphatic speech are almost identical in the two languages.

(6) Difference in the representation of phonemes in the written language. This results in the error that a learner, who has been learning mostly through reading, pronounces wrongly the phonemes that are represented by some particular letter symbol in his native language and indeed sometimes phonemes that are not pronounced in the target language. An example of the former case is that instead of pronouncing a ə in English words in positions where no other vowel should be pronounced, Czechs and surely native speakers of many other languages pronounce the sound usually represented in their native language by the letter signal standing, as it were, for ə in the particular English word. An example of the latter case is that the Czechs pronounce a l in such words as half or a w in such words as answer, and almost always a r before consonants.

In order to meet all these potential cases of interference, and to predict the errors and to find the most effective methods of overcoming the inhibiting factors of the native language and internalizing the new system in the learner's mind, it is necessary for the linguist to contrast the two systems of phonemes and point out those which occur in one language while they do not in the other, to contrast the combinatory patterns of sounds of the two languages, the limitations of occurrence of separate phonemes, the allophones of the corresponding phonemes of the two languages, the different patterns of phonological neutralization and the intonational and rhythmic patterns.

It is also necessary to treat contrastively each separate phoneme of the target language. In doing so the following procedure was applied in my own work. All allophones of the phoneme under study were described and contrasted with the allophones of the corresponding phoneme, if any, in the native language. Further, the status of the phoneme in the system of phonemes is described and studied from its functional aspects, including the functional load in confrontation with the corresponding phoneme of the native language, if any. The combinatory patterns and limitations of occurrence are described and contrasted. All predictable difficulties for the Czech learner are discussed, and materials and methods for effective exercises are suggested. All letter signals representing the phoneme under study are listed.

Theoretical conclusions concerning the predictability of errors are of value only if they are backed by empirical data. In this direction I have been able to work out a test of perception presenting pairs of words differing only in the one phonological feature that has theoretically been found liable to cause errors to Czech learners. My work with these tests, which was recently started, has not proceeded so far as to enable me to give here any meaningful figures but seems to confirm most of the theoretical conclusions.

The Yugoslav Serbo-Croatian—English Contrastive Project

RUDOLF FILIPOVIĆ

It is common ground that one of the major problems in the learning of the second language is the interference caused by the structural differences between the primary language of the learner, the source language (L_S), and the target language (L_T). This problem has been largely neglected in the teaching of foreign languages.

C. C. Fries as far back as 1945 expressed an idea which in a way predicted contrastive analysis: 'The most efficient materials are those that are based upon a scientific description of the language to be learned, carefully compared with a parallel description of the native language of the learner.'[1] W. F. Mackey has stressed the importance of the contrastive description of L_S and L_T for pedagogical purposes. 'Differential description,' says Mackey, 'is of particular interest to language teaching because many of the difficulties in learning a second language are due to the fact that it differs from the first. So that if we subtract the characteristics of the first language from those of the second, what presumably remains is a list of the learner's difficulties.'[2]

It is assumed that the areas of interference can be predicted on the basis of contrastive, or differential, analysis. A contrastive analysis is an attempt to predict and elucidate the reactions of learners in a given contact situation. The learner's knowledge of the source language (L_S) affects the learning of the target language (L_T). Where structures of L_S and L_T coincide formally and semantically the learning process will be easier, and where they differ the learning process will be inhibited.

The primary aim and the main objective of the Yugoslav Serbo-Croatian–English Contrastive Project[3] is an examination of all systemic

[1] C. C. Fries, *Teaching and Learning English as a Foreign Language*, Ann Arbor, 1945, p. 9.
[2] W. F. Mackey, *Language Teaching Analysis*, London, 1965, p. 80.
[3] Rudolf Filipović, *The Organization and Objectives of the Project. The Yugoslav Contrastive Analysis Project – Serbo-Croatian and English*, Zagreb, 1968.

[107]

differences and similarities that exist between Serbo-Croatian and English at all levels of linguistic description. A detailed contrastive investigation of the two languages is expected to provide sufficient information about their elements and structures to enable comprehensive and useful comparison. The results of the analysis and of the structural comparison obtained with the tools of modern linguistic science will serve as a sound foundation for improved teaching of English in Yugoslavia and of Serbo-Croatian in America and Great Britain.

It is hoped that the work, undertaken by leading Yugoslav scholars, experts in both English and Serbo-Croatian, will also add to linguistic theory and practice in this field and that the results of their work will provide further insight into the linguistic structure of the two languages. The final product, it is hoped, will make a valuable contribution to the growing body of contrastive linguistics.

The Project will thus benefit directly not only practical language teachers but equally those interested in linguistic theory and practice.

The contrastive analysis of Serbo-Croatian and English is being carried out at four linguistic levels: (a) phonology, (b) syntax, (c) morphology with word-formation, (d) lexis. The structure of English has been divided into about forty categories in its phonological, morphological, syntactical and lexical aspects.

In phonology the following topics will be analysed: (a) stress, (b) rhythm, (c) intonation, (d) the vowel system, (e) the system of consonants, (f) the morpho-phonemics of Serbo-Croatian and English.

In syntax the analysis is focused on the sentence as the point of departure. The following topics are being discussed: (a) subject, (b) the predicate of the type 'verb + predicative', (c) the predicate of the type 'verb + object', (d) simple sentence. These topics will be further subdivided. So, for instance, the topic 'Subject' will be subdivided into: (1) noun and nominal sequence, (2) verb and verbal sequence, (3) pronoun and pronominal sequence, (4) complex, (5) clause.

The following topics dealing with parts of speech are being analysed: the noun (number and gender), nominalization, articles, pronouns, adjectives, numerals and expressions of quantity, the verb (aspectives, voice, modal verbs, imperative and its periphrases, formal expression of (a) present time, (b) simultaneous action, (c) general time, (d) past time, (e) future time).

In morphology comparison will be discussed, while word-formation will cover the methods of forming words: composition, derivation and conversion.

In lexis we plan to determine contrastive patterning in semantically corresponding clusters, in synonymy groupings, in Latin-root words, in frequency correspondences, etc.

We have planned to write three Research Guides for Project Workers. The first dealing with matters of grammar (morphology and syntax)[1] is already being used by our researchers; the other two will be written soon, before we start our analysis on the other two levels: phonology and lexis.

The analysis begins with the target language structures (categories, word classes, constructions) which are presented in terms of a given description to obtain topics for contrasting.

Two types of relationship between the structures of Serbo-Croatian and English are taken into consideration: (*a*) the given structure occurs in English but it does not occur in Serbo-Croatian, (*b*) the given structure occurs in both languages. If the given structure occurs only in English and not in Serbo-Croatian, the learner's knowledge of Serbo-Croatian will neither inhibit nor facilitate the acquisition of the English structure (e.g. the article in English versus no article in Serbo-Croatian).

If the given structure occurs in both languages, they partially overlap, formally and semantically. The cases of partial overlap are the primary concern of contrastive analysis since it is in these cases that the Serbo-Croatian learner of English will be tempted to assume that the overlap is total and will distort the English structure in an attempt to secure conformity with its Serbo-Croatian counterpart. This is the case with verbal tenses, adjectives, possessives, and numerous other structures.

Two possibilities exist in cases of overlap: first, the English structure may have a wider range than the corresponding Serbo-Croatian structure; second, the range of the English structure may be narrower than that of the corresponding Serbo-Croatian structure.

When analysing the possessive adjectives contrastively, Serbo-Croatian vs. English, we have noticed that their range of application in English extends beyond their range of application in Serbo-Croatian and that it covers, among other things, part of the area occupied by the Serbo-Croatian personal pronouns.

On the other hand, a contrastive analysis of reflexivity in Serbo-Croatian and English has shown that Serbo-Croatian is richer in the use of reflexive forms than English.

In both cases the analysis starts from English, outlines the syntactic field of the English structure, contrasts it with the Serbo-Croatian equiva-

---

[1] W. Nemser and V. Ivir, 'Research Guide for Project Workers. I. Morphology and Syntax', *The Yugoslav Serbo-Croatian–English Contrastive Project. A. Reports*, 1, Zagreb, 1969.

lent to note the area of overlap, and lists possible areas of interference. Where the Serbo-Croatian structure has a wider range, the remaining instances of its usage will be analysed in connection with the description of certain other structures in English.

In our Research Guide for Project Workers dealing with syntax and morphology the following analytical procedures are recommended:

(1) The analyst begins with the description of the English structure.

(2) Next, formal-semantic correspondences in Serbo-Croatian are sought. Since English and Serbo-Croatian are sufficiently related to enable us to set up our categories in terms of a metalanguage common to both, correspondences should first be sought in Serbo-Croatian categories of the same rank. After that, correspondences of other ranks, possibly even at other levels, should be examined.

(3) Once the correspondences have been established in Serbo-Croatian, they are analysed to see how they differ from their English counterparts. This is the process of contrastive, or differential, analysis proper.

(4) Predictions for learning are made on the basis of such contrastive, differential analysis. Then tests are devised to check on the accuracy of these predictions.

(5) Teaching strategy and materials are planned in the light of the predictions and tests results.

Individual studies which follow the above analytical procedures will consist of three sections: (a) a short summary, (b) the actual analysis of the topic in question, and (c) a section on pedagogical implications. The study summary describes the methodological approach employed in the research and the principal results obtained.

The work in progress appears in the Project publications, which consist of three series: A. Reports, B. Studies, C. Pedagogical Materials. The first volume of our publications, under the title of *The Organization and Objectives of the Project*,[1] appeared in 1968. It is devoted to general information on the Project with a description of the Project design and a list of Project personnel with their organizational affiliation and their Project responsibilities.

The *Reports* of Series A contain progress reports on individual studies. In Volume I[2] reports on Nominal Group,[3] Prepositional Phrases,[4] Inver-

---

[1] See p. 107, n. 3.
[2] *The Yugoslav Serbo-Croatian–English Contrastive Project. A. Reports*, 1. ed. Rudolf Filipović, Zagreb, 1969.
[3] Vjekoslav Suzanić, 'The Nominal Group in English and Serbo-Croatian', *A. Reports*, 1, pp. 51–62.
[4] Ranko Bugarski, 'Prepositional Phrases in English and Serbo-Croatian', *A. Reports*, 1, p. 25.

sion,[1] Gender,[2] Adjectives,[3] Aspectives in English,[4] Modal Verbs,[5] and Derivation[6] have been printed. In the same volume in addition to the reports there are two more contributions, *Research Guide for Project Workers. I. Morphology and Syntax*[7] and *Direction and Continuity in Contrastive Analysis.*[8]

Series B consists principally of the studies produced by individual researchers. It also contains articles of theoretical interest by Project members. Volume 1 of *Studies*[9] contains the following articles: William Nemser, *Approximative Systems of Foreign Language Learners*;[10] Vladimir Ivir, *Contrasting via Translation: Formal Correspondence vs. Translation Equivalence*;[11] Leonardo Spalatin, *Approach to Contrastive Analysis*;[12] Rudolf Filipović, *The Choice of the Corpus for a Contrastive Analysis of Serbo-Croatian and English.*[13]

A special issue of our publications entitled *Prilozi i grada*,[14] written in Serbo-Croatian,[15] summarizes the results of the work on the Project over the three-year period (1966–8). This volume is meant for Yugoslav readers who do not read English but are interested in contrastive analysis of Serbo-Croatian and other foreign languages.

Series C, *Pedagogical Materials*, will present specimen teaching materials demonstrating the applicability of the findings of the contrastive research to the development of teaching materials. No work has been done on this level: we have to wait for the first findings of the contrastive research which will appear in *Studies*, in Section (*c*) of each study.

The first two problems that we faced at the very beginning of our work

[1] Ljiljana Bibović, 'On Inversion in English and Serbo-Croatian', *A. Reports*, 1, pp. 15–24.
[2] Dora Maček, 'Gender in English and Serbo-Croatian', *A. Reports*, 1, pp. 45–50.
[3] Vladimir Ivir, 'An Outline for the Contrastive Analysis of English and Serbo-Croatian Adjectives', *A. Reports*, 1, pp. 31–8.
[4] Mira Vlatković, 'Elements of Aspectives in English', *A. Reports*, 1, pp. 63–70.
[5] Damir Kalogjera, 'A Survey of Grammatical Characteristics of the English Modal Verbs with regard to Interference Problems', *A. Reports*, 1, pp. 39–44.
[6] Željko Bujas, 'Brief Outline of Planned Work on Derivation', *A. Reports*, 1, pp. 26–30.
[7] Written by William Nemser and Vladimir Ivir, *A. Reports*, 1, pp. 3–8.
[8] Written by Ranko Bugarski, *A. Reports*, 1, pp. 9–14.
[9] *The Yugoslav Serbo-Croatian–English Contrastive Project. B. Studies*, 1, ed. Rudolf Filipović, Zagreb, 1969.
[10] *B. Studies*, 1, pp. 3–12. [11] *Ibid.*, pp. 13–25.
[12] *Ibid.*, p. 26. [13] *Ibid.*, pp. 37–46.
[14] *Jugoslavenski projekt za konstrastivnu analizu srpskohrvatskog i engleskog jezika. Prilozi i grada*, 1, Uredio Rudolf Filipović, Zagreb, 1969.
[15] Rudolf Filipović, Početne faze rada na projektu Kontrastivna analiza hrvatskosrpskog i engleskog jezika', *Prilozi i grada*, 1, pp. 3–25. Pavle Ivić, 'Nekoliko reči o problemima metoda', *Ibid.*, pp. 26–9. Ljubomir Mihailović; 'Kontrastivna analiza fonoloških sistema', *Ibid.*, pp. 30–4. Željko Bujas, 'Primjena kompjutera i fleksorajtera u radu na projektu Kontrastivna analiza hrvatskosrpskog i engleskog jezika', *Ibid.* pp. 35–59.

were the method and the corpus. Obviously, the choice of the method determined whether a specific corpus was needed or not.

The problem of the method was discussed in the earliest stages of our work on the Project.[1] One of three approaches was possible: traditional, structuralist, or generative. Discussing this question Professor Pavle Ivić stated that our progressive orientation should dictate the choice of the most modern, i.e. generative-transformational, approach. However, the situation in the field forced us to compromise, to combine classical structuralism with the elements of the generative approach.[2]

After having examined several contrastive studies now available we found that none employs a specific and consistent method that might be regarded as *the* method of contrastive analysis.[3] These considerations have prompted us to seek a method, or a combination of methods, that will yield not only theoretical but also practical results. The practical results must be usable in developing better teaching materials and techniques. This will be possible only if they are presented in a form that an average reader of our projected monograph (*Contrastive Analysis of Serbo-Croatian and English*) can understand.

In order to fulfil all the requirements of the contrastive description of Serbo-Croatian and English it was decided to adopt the translation method based on a corpus of examples. This choice then led naturally to another problem: that of the corpus.

At the beginning we planned to build our own corpus on some specific principles.[4] It became, however, quite clear that it would be rather difficult, if not impossible, to build such a large corpus within the limited time and with the resources that we had at our disposal, and that consequently we would have to use an existing corpus and a computer and other data processing devices.[5] There are, at present, two large corpora: one built on British material, spoken and written, *A Survey of English Usage*,[6] compiled

---

[1] Rudolf Filipović, 'Contrastive Analysis of Serbo-Croatian and English', *Studia Romanica et Anglica Zagrabiensia*, 23, Zagreb, 1967, pp. 5–27. Leonardo Spalatin, 'Contrastive Methods', *SRAZ*, 23, Zagreb, 1967, pp. 29–48. Željko Bujas, 'Concordancing as a Method in Contrastive Analysis', *SRAZ*, 23, Zagreb, 1967, pp. 49–62.

[2] Pavle Ivić, 'Nekoliko reči o problemima metoda', *Jugoslavenski projekt za kontrastivnu analizu srpskohrvatskog i engleskog jezika. Prilozi i grada*, 1, Zagreb, 1969, pp. 26–9.

[3] Rudolf Filipović, 'Contrastive Analysis of Serbo-Croatian and English', *SRAZ*, 23, Zagreb, 1967, p. 10.

[4] *Ibid.*, p. 26.

[5] Željko Bujas, 'Concordancing as a Method in Contrastive Analysis', *SRAZ*, 23, Zagreb, 1967, 49–62.

[6] R. Quirk, 'Towards a Description of English Usage', *Transactions of the Philological Society*, Blackwell, Oxford, 1961, pp. 40–61. R. Quirk, 'On English Usage', *Journal of the Royal Society of Arts*, 114, London, 1966, pp. 837–51.

under the leadership of Professor Randolph Quirk (University College, London), and another one built on American material, only written, *The Brown Corpus* (short for the *Standard Sample of Present-Day Edited American English*)[1] selected and prepared for computer-processing by W. N. Francis and Henry Kučera of Brown University.

By its composition and size the former corpus would meet the requirements of our Project. Two main reasons have prevented us from choosing it: (a) Professor Quirk's corpus is not readily accessible since it does not exist in printed form; (b) it is not designed for computer processing. Those were the two major reasons for our decision to work with the American Brown Corpus, whose most serious drawback is that it does not cover the spoken language.[2] This corpus is now available on magnetic tape for computer processing.

The text of the Brown Corpus has been obtained by running the tape through the computer, which has printed the entire text in its orthographic form. For technical and financial reasons we have shortened the Brown Corpus by half. After reduction by one half, with emphasis given to dialogues and letters to the editor (as these two categories come perhaps closest to the free style of expression that we need most in our corpus), the thus abbreviated corpus has been translated into Serbo-Croatian by regionally representative translators, selected to be representative of the three major regional variants of Serbo-Croatian (western, central and eastern). It is thus hoped that the Brown Corpus translation into Serbo-Croatian will display the greatest possible number of features of all variants.

It was clear to us from the beginning that the contrastive analysis of the two languages (Serbo-Croatian and English) would require two corpora of equal size and composition which would be translated into the respective languages. This would enable us to examine each phenomenon in both languages from the point of view of its translation. This idea had to be given up, however, for several reasons, and it was eventually decided to work with only one corpus and its Serbo-Croatian translation.

Obviously, the Brown Corpus and its Serbo-Croatian translation cannot provide all the elements needed in the analysis: we have therefore decided to have another, control corpus, which will be smaller and less representa-

---

[1] The main information on the sources for this corpus can be found in W. N. Francis, *Manual of Information to Accompany a Standard Sample of Present-Day Edited American English for Use with Digital Computers*, Department of Linguistics, Brown University, Providence, Rhode Island, 1964.

[2] Rudolf Filipović, 'The Choice of the Corpus for a Contrastive Analysis of Serbo-Croatian and English', *The Yugoslav Serbo-Croatian–English Contrastive Project. B. Studies*, 1, Zagreb, 1969, pp. 37–46.

tive than the shortened version of the Brown Corpus. It consists of a few Serbo-Croatian novels and their translation into English by native speakers of English. So our complete corpus consists of twice 500,000 words (the Brown Corpus with its Serbo-Croatian translation) plus twice 150,000 words (a smaller Control Corpus – Serbo-Croatian originals and English translation), or a grand total of some 1,300,000 words of running text.

On the basis of this big corpus processed by the IBM 360 computer in the Zagreb Municipal Computer Centre we shall obtain the normal and the reverse KWIC concordances of both the English and Serbo-Croatian corpora. By merging these monolingual concordances we shall get contrastive concordances,[1] which will be used by the Project analysts in their research.

This Project involves the cooperation of Yugoslav and American scholars. In its work on this Project the Institute of Linguistics of the University of Zagreb enjoys the cooperation of the Center for Applied Linguistics in Washington. The Project is directed by Dr Rudolf Filipović, Professor of English and Director of the Institute of Linguistics, and coordinated by the Center for Applied Linguistics represented by Dr William Nemser, Director of the Center's Foreign Language Program.

The Project is financed jointly by the governments of Yugoslavia and the United States, and by the Ford Foundation.

The final product of this Project will be a book on the contrastive analysis of Serbo-Croatian and English, in which the results of the individual studies will be collated and summarized. It will contain a sample set of teaching materials illustrating the applicability of the results of the studies to course development and to the teaching of all aspects of English language structure to students in all age groups and at all levels of proficiency. The book will also contain one section concerning the pedagogical implications of the teaching of Serbo-Croatian to speakers of English.

[1] Technical details of how the computer is being used in our Project have been given in the paper 'Computers in the Yugoslav Serbo-Croat/English Contrastive Analysis Project', read by Dr Željko Bujas at the International Conference on Computational Linguistics, held in Stockholm in 1969.

Over-indulgence and under-representation–
aspects of mother-tongue interference

E. A. LEVENSTON

INTRODUCTION

One feature of non-native use of a second language, or L2, is the excessive use ('over-indulgence') of clause (or group) structures which closely resemble translation-equivalents in the mother tongue, or L1, to the exclusion of other structures ('under-representation') which are less like anything in L1. 'Closely resemble' can be more precisely defined as 'with translation-equivalents which correspond at the level of group (or word) as well as clause'; 'less like' means with translation equivalents which correspond at the level of clause (or group) only'.

Although the L2 clause structure produced by group level translation may be completely acceptable, both grammatically and lexically, it can still produce effects by no means intended by the user: verbosity, formality, informality, and so on. The purpose of this paper is twofold; to attempt a taxonomy of these different effects, and to suggest a method of predicting them. The need for such an approach has recently been formulated in these words: 'to be complete, a contrastive analysis must go beyond the mere comparison of rule systems, it must also take into consideration the distribution of the rules with respect to register and style'.[1]

For ease of presentation, all structures will be exemplified rather than formally defined. For formal definition, any system of grammatical analysis would suffice that gave an adequate account of surface structure. OI stands for over-indulgence, UR for under-representation. In practice, under-representation may actually amount to complete absence.[2] All examples

---

[1] G. Nickel and K. H. Wagner, 'Contrastive linguistics and language teaching', *IRAL* VI (1968) 3: 233–57.
[2] This is also noted by L. Dušková, 'On sources of errors in foreign language learning', *IRAL*, VII (1969) 1: 29, who says of one construction that it 'will not present problems on the production level simply because hardly any learner will spontaneously use it'.

are taken, if possible, from my own research in the problems of Hebrew-speakers learning English and from their work in free composition; not translation. I have also hazarded a few guesses about similar phenomena that can be inferred from contrastive analyses published of other pairs of languages and language-learning situations.

TAXONOMY

1. *Formality*

Of two L2 structures, learners will prefer the more formal:

(*a*) OI   It is obvious that they... ⎱ muvan me'elav shehem...
     UR   Obviously they... ⎰

(*b*) OI   I think not   ⎱ ani hoshev shelo
     UR   I don't think so ⎰

(*c*) OI   He said that he agreed ⎱ amar shehu maskim
     UR   He said he agreed   ⎰

And similarly with relative clauses, where Hebrew-speakers will always prefer some explicit relative pronoun. This phenomenon is presumably not restricted to Hebrew-speaking learners, but would occur with speakers of any language which has no contact clauses – embedded sentences un-marked by relative pronoun or subordinate conjunction – e.g. French and German.

Kufner has also commented on a difference between English and German which affects the level of formality of English-speakers' German and German-speakers' English. The use of inversion instead of 'if' in English conditional clauses is less frequent than omission of 'wenn' in German. 'Most of our students seem to feel that such inverted clauses are old-fashioned and they tend to avoid them at least in speaking'.[1] The reference is to English students learning German. Presumably German students learning English use inversion to excess, which may help to explain the sometimes excessive formality of German speakers of English.

(*d*) OI   It is I   ⎱ Ze ani
     UR   It is me ⎰

Hebrew-speakers also answer questions like 'Who's there?' or 'Who did it?' with 'I'.

---

[1] Herbert L. Kufner, *The Grammatical Structures of English and German*, Chicago, 1962, p. 80.

2. Verbosity

Of two L2 structures learners will prefer the wordier, the more verbose, which would be avoided by writers who obey George Orwell's third law: 'If it is possible to cut a word out, always cut it out.'[1]

(*a*) OR There is no possibility for me to... ⎱ ein li shum
    UI I cannot possibly... ⎰ efsharut...

(*b*) OR The thought that I will see you... ⎱ ha mahsheva she'ani
    UI The thought of seeing you... ⎰ er'e otkha

(*c*) OI After I had finished and I had understood... ⎱ aharei
    UR After I had finished and understood... ⎰ shegamarti vehevanti

And many similar structures where English has greater possibilities for ellipsis than Hebrew.

3. Informality

Of two L2 structures, learners will prefer the more informal:

(*a*) OI They thought that he was innocent ⎱ hashvu shehaya
    UR They thought him innocent ⎰ haf mipesha

(*b*) OI If he was here ⎱ im hu haya kan
    UR If he were here ⎰

(*c*) OI If I would have known I would have gone ⎱ im hayiti
    UR If I had known, I would have gone ⎰ yodea, hayiti holekh

4. Sub-standard

Of the two L2 structures, learners will prefer the sub-standard. This of course will normally be treated as an error and corrected in the normal course of teaching. The point I wish to make is that it may arise from mother-tongue interference, and not from contact with sub-standard speakers.

(*a*) OI I don't see nothing ⎱ ani lo ro'e shum davar
    UR I don't see anything ⎰

(*b*) OI My husband, he's an engineer ⎱ ba'ali hu mehandes
    UR My husband is an engineer ⎰

Although this last example is not exactly sub-standard, the greater prevalence of disjunctive structures in Hebrew may lead to a preference for disjunction in English – and this is a feature of sub-standard speech.

[1] George Orwell 'Politics and the English Language', in *Collected Essays*, London, 1961, p. 350.

5. Dialect

Of two L2 structures, learners will prefer one with greater frequency of occurrence in a particular *standard* dialect:

OI   Did you finish already? (American) ⎱
UR   Have you finished already? (British) ⎰ gamarta kvar?

A similar situation is discussed by Kufner in his analysis of the difference between English past simple and present perfect and their equivalents in German. Any use in speech of 'ich sah' rather than 'ich habe gesehen' gives a 'hochdeutsch' flavour to one's German.[1]

6. Under-differentiation

Where two L2 structures are slightly different in meaning and use, learners will generalize one to cover the uses of both. As long as the difference is contextually irrelevant, the foreign learner's preference may pass unnoticed:

(*a*) OI   I like to sing in the bath ⎱ ani ohev lashir ba'ambatia
     UR   I like singing in the bath ⎰

(*b*) OI   I heard her singing in the bath ⎱ shama'ti ota shara
     UR   I heard her sing in the bath ⎰ ba'ambatia

(*c*) OI   He said he will come ⎱ amar sheyavo
     UR   He said he would come ⎰

Actually, if teachers insist on the rigid application of sequence-of-tense rules, 'he said he will come' will be treated as an error. The point is that whatever attitude one adopts as a pedagogue to the two systems of tense-sequence in English, there is only one system in Hebrew.

In this connection, one might mention the different possibilities for adjective position in French and Italian, either before or after the noun, contrasting with fixed position in English. English-speaking learners of these languages, once they have mastered the more frequent, post-nominal position probably tend to use it on all occasions, not always without mishap.

Similarly, Bolinger contrasts the English passive with the choice in Spanish between a passive and a reflexive construction. Spanish uses the passive 'substantially less than English does...It is less favoured than English for some purposes, in spite of the fact that there are countless tokens that are impeccable'. Presumably, then, English-speakers learning

[1] Kufner, *Grammatical Structures of English and German*, p. 88.

Spanish may use the passive in Spanish more than Spanish speakers, and not always impeccably.[1]

7. *Interchangeability*

Where two L2 structures are more or less interchangeable, the preference of foreign learners for one structure rather than another may pass completely unnoticed. However, their English will not be native-speakers' English as far as the *frequency* of particular structures is concerned.

(*a*) OI Perhaps he will come ⎫
  UR He may come ⎬ ulai yavo

(*b*) OI A book was given to him ⎫
  UR He was given a book ⎬ nitan lo sefer

(*c*) OI He behaved in a ridiculous way/ ⎫
    with intelligence ⎪
  UR He behaved ridiculously/ ⎬ hu hitnaheg hetsura
    intelligently ⎪ meguhekhet/
     ⎭ besekhel

Hebrew has no morphological equivalent of equal generality to '-ly' as an adverbial suffix in English. The various Hebrew substitutes may or may not work in any given instance.

8. *Archaism*

Of two L2 structures, learners will prefer the more archaic. Like sub-standard forms, archaisms are usually corrected in the normal course of teaching. Sometimes, however, the line is not so easy to draw:

OI He asked that I might come and see him
UR He asked me to come and see him

This is not from my own experience with Hebrew-speakers but is quoted from a study of common errors in Gold Coast English.[2] The authors quote the first sentence, with a translation-equivalent in Twi, and add that such sentences 'although correct 300 years ago, are now found only in schoolboys' translations from the Latin'.

Finally, a complete theoretical analysis of all possible inter-language relationships involved in this phenomenon would also have to take into account the effect of diglossia, with L1 or L2, on the language learning situation. This has been missing from my empirical statement of the

[1] See Dwight Bolinger, 'Transformation: structural translation', in *Acta Linguistica Hafniensia* IX (1966), 2: 130–44.
[2] P. P. Brown and J. Scragg, *Common Errors in Gold Coast English*, Macmillan, London, 1953, pp. 90–7.

relation between English and Hebrew, since in neither of them does diglossia obtain. Some hints as to the effect of Greek diglossia on English learners can perhaps be inferred from Householder's account of the situation.[1] The frequency of participial structures in Katharevousa that he quotes is most un-English. English Greeks would presumably tend in this respect to sound more demotic.

I have also omitted from this analysis any account of those L1 clause structures which, if translated group by group into L2, produce a perfectly grammatical L2 clause *with a meaning entirely different from the one intended*, e.g. Hebrew 'hu omed ledaber' – English 'he is standing to speak' (instead of 'he is about to speak'). These phenomena are of course 'errors', and can be found in all published contrastive analyses.[2]

Prediction

To be honest, I am not sure which of the examples quoted were predicted by the analysis and which were brought to my attention in classroom practice and marking written work. Nevertheless, the following method is proposed as a discovery procedure by means of which a linguist working with adequate descriptions of two languages, but no classroom teaching experience, could predict the occurrence of such features.

List the structures of L2 and their translation equivalents in L1.[3] When no L1 structure is equivalent at group level, translate the commonest L1 equivalent back into L2, group for group. If the result is acceptable in L2, consider the relationship between the two L2 structures in the light of the taxonomy here suggested.

Example 1

English		Hebrew
S(pronoun) P^F (seem...)		P(nidme) A(pronominal)
P^{NF} (to...)	→	S (clause)
I seem to remember...	→	nidme li she'ani zokher...

Group-level translation of the Hebrew back into English: It seems to me that I remember.

---

[1] Fred W. Householder, Jr., 'Greek Diglossia', in *Report on the 13th Annual Round Table Meeting on Linguistics and Language Studies*, Georgetown University Press, 1963, pp. 109–29.

[2] An interesting example, deriving from differences in the position of markers of negation, is quoted in Afia Dil, 'Teaching Bengali to Urdu Speakers', *Pakistani Linguistics* (1966), Lahore, 1963, pp. 165–77.

[3] See E. A. Levenston, 'The translation-paradigm', *IRAL* III (August 1965), 3: 221–5.

Prediction: Hebrew-speakers will prefer the more verbose, wordier English structure (category 2).

This example, and the formulation of the analytical procedure, can handle differences in clause structure; by substituting 'group' for 'clause' and 'word' for 'group', differences at the level of group can be similarly handled:

Example 2

	English		Hebrew
d¹ d² h		→	h q
such a man		→	'ish kaze

Word level translation: a man like that.

Prediction: Hebrew-speakers will use the somewhat more informal English pattern, though the absence of 'such' from their English may not be noticed (category 3, or 7).

Conclusion

The importance of this kind of analysis lies in the help it can give to advanced learners. The goal of foreign language teaching is sometimes thought to be reached when the learner has achieved mechanical mastery of the structures of the second language. Any further refinement of choice among these structures is regarded as stylistics. And this is outside the scope of contrastive analysis if conceived as primarily concerned with the prediction and description of errors.[1] If the advanced learner uses structures which are acceptable, even though in one way or another inappropriate, nobody offers any guidance. He will possibly not even realize that further instruction is desirable. Analysis along the lines suggested here may provide the form which such instruction could most usefully take.

[1] 'The value of contrastive analysis in the preparation of teaching materials is generally recognized both as a means of preventing and of remedying errors', L. Dušková 'Sources of errors in foreign language learning', p. 29. See also Robert P. Stockwell, J. Donald Bower and John W. Manlin, *The Grammatical Structures of English and Spanish*, Chicago, 1965, *passim*, for the use of 'typical errors'.